**W9-CBU-240**

# A Travel ✦ Guide to ANCIENT POMPEII

## By Don Nardo

**LUCENT BOOKS**

*An imprint of Thomson Gale, a part of The Thomson Corporation*

THOMSON

GALE

Detroit • New York • San Francisco • San Diego • New Haven, Conn. • Waterville, Maine • London • Munich

LIBRARY OF CONGRESS CATALOGING-IN-PUBLICATION DATA

Nardo, Don, 1947–
    Ancient Pompeii / by Don Nardo.
      p. cm. — (A travel guide to)
    Includes bibliographical references and index.
    ISBN 1-59018-457-2 (hardcover : alk. paper)
    1. Pompeii (Extinct city)—Guidebooks—Juvenile literature. 2. Pompeii (Extinct city)—
Social life and customs—Juvenile literature. I. Title. II. Series: Travel guide (Lucent Books)
    DG70.P7N37 2004
    937'.7—dc22
                                                                                    2004014886

Printed in the United States of America

# Contents

# Foreword

Travel can be a unique way to learn about oneself and other cultures. The esteemed American writer and historian, John Hope Franklin, poetically expressed his conviction in the value of travel by urging, "We must go beyond textbooks, go out into the bypaths and untrodden depths of the wilderness and travel and explore and tell the world the glories of our journey." The message communicated by this eloquent entreaty is clear: The value of travel is to temper one's imagination about a place and its people with reality, and instead of thinking how things may be, to be able to experience them as they really are.

Franklin's voice is not alone in his summons for students to "travel and explore." He is joined by a stentorian chorus of thinkers that includes former president John F. Kennedy, who established the Peace Corps to facilitate cross-cultural understandings between Americans and citizens of other lands. Ideas about the benefits of travel do not spring only from contemporary times. The ancient Greek historian Herodotus journeyed to foreign lands for the purpose of immersing himself in unfa-miliar cultural traditions. In this way, he believed, he might gain a first-hand understanding of people and ways of life in other places.

The joys, insights, and satisfaction that travelers derive from their journeys are not limited to cultural understanding. Travel has the added value of enhancing the traveler's inner self by expanding his or her range of experiences. Writer Paul Tournier concurs that, "The real meaning of travel, like that of a conversation by the fireside, is the discovery of oneself through contact with other people."

The Lucent Books Travel Guide series enlivens history by introducing a new and innovative style and format. Each volume in the series presents the history of a preeminent historical travel destination written in the casual style and format of a travel guide. Whether providing a tour of fifth-century B.C. Athens, Renaissance Florence, or Shakespeare's London, each book describes a city or area at its cultural peak and orients readers to only those places and activities that are known to have existed at that time.

A high level of authenticity is achieved in the Travel Guide series. Each book is written in the present tense and addresses the reader as a prospective foreign traveler. The sense of authenticity is further achieved, whenever possible, by the inclusion of descriptive quotations by contemporary writers who knew the place; information on fascinating historical sites; and travel tips meant to explain unusual cultural idiosyncrasies that give depth and texture to all great cultural centers. Even shopping details, such as where to buy an ermine-trimmed gown, or a much-needed house slave, are included to inform readers of what items were sought after throughout history.

Looked at collectively, this series presents an appealing presentation of many of the cultural and social highlights of Western civilization. The collection also provides a framework for discussion about the larger historical currents that dominated not only each travel destination but countries and entire continents as well. Each book is customized by the author to bring to the fore the most important and most interesting characteristics that define each title. High standards of scholarship are assured in the series by the generous peppering of relevant quotes and extensive bibliographies. These tools provide readers a scholastic standard for their own research as well as a guide to direct them to other books, periodicals, and Web sites that will provide them greater breadth and detail.

# A Note to the Reader

This volume takes the novel approach of examining the history, society, and culture of the ancient Roman city of Pompeii in the format of a modern travel guide. On the one hand, this is an innovative and entertaining way to learn about ancient Roman history, architecture, art, customs, lifestyles, and ideas. The fictional author of the guide speaks directly to the reader, as if Pompeii is still a living, breathing city. This gives the text an immediacy that the average historical narrative lacks.

On the other hand, this unusual approach does entail some technical difficulties that do not exist in straightforward history texts. Perhaps the most obvious of these difficulties is that a number of accepted conventions of dating and measurement have changed over the centuries. The ancients obviously did not employ modern

inches, feet, meters, miles, kilometers, and so forth, but rather had their own units of measure. But these ancient units are now unfamiliar to all but a handful of scholars. To make the text more understandable to today's readers, therefore, this book uses modern units of measurement, including miles, square miles, and degrees of temperature.

Dates present an even more conspicuous obstacle. Most history books automatically use the designation B.C., meaning "Before Christ" and A.D., denoting the Christian era. In the standard B.C.-A.D. scheme, the year in which Pompeii's all-stone amphitheater (Rome's first) was inaugurated, is denoted as 80 B.C., or eighty years before the beginning of the Christian era. The problem is that the B.C.-A.D. dating system did not exist in ancient times; Christian scholars introduced it in early medieval times. The people of the ancient Mediterranean world had a number of different dating systems of their own, which often existed side by side. Thus, if this travel guide had actually been written in ancient times, the author would have used one of the dating systems then accepted. However, using such an obscure and unfamiliar system in a modern book would not be very practical; so for the sake of clarity and convenience, this volume utilizes the standard B.C.-A.D. dating system.

Outside of these conventions, all aspects of this travel guide are authentic. They are based on evidence derived from surviving ancient literary texts and studies made by archaeologists and other scholars of paintings, sculptures, buildings, tools, weapons, coins, and other ancient artifacts. All of the places and sites described were real. And the ruins of most of these sites still exist in Italy, where modern tourists flock to see them each year.

## Haunted by the Ghosts of the Past

In addition to adopting a dating system for ancient Pompeii that is familiar to modern readers, the author of this book had to choose a date for the writing of

*An outside stairway leads to the top of the seating section of the stone amphitheater at Pompeii, built in 80 B.C.*

Campania

the fictional travel guide. He decided on the year A.D. 78 for two principal reasons. First, by that time Pompeii had been a thriving town for several centuries, having been occupied and controlled by a number of different Italian peoples before becoming a Roman city. So its somewhat cosmopolitan history, institutions, and customs were by then well established. This better allows the reader to appreciate the city's colorful background and to

learn about its structures, arts, economy, and lifestyles during the early years of the Roman Empire (which had been established about a century before).

The second reason for dating this travel guide to A.D. 78 is that it makes the book a sort of snapshot of the city on the eve of its total destruction. As many people today—even those who know little about ancient history—are aware, on August 24, A.D. 79, the volcano Mt. Vesuvius, situated only a few miles from Pompeii, erupted violently.

At the time, the noted Roman naturalist and scholar Pliny the Elder and his nephew, Pliny the Younger, were living in the area (the Gulf of Cumae, today known as the Bay of Naples) and witnessed the eruption. The elder Pliny actually placed himself in harm's way in a daring effort to learn about a rare natural disaster up close. "My uncle . . . saw at once that it [the eruption] was important enough for a closer inspection," the younger Pliny later wrote. "He ordered a boat to be made ready, telling me that I could come with him if I wished. I replied that I preferred to go on with my studies." The older man then hurried away, "steering his course straight for the danger zone. He was entirely fearless, describing each new movement and phase of the eruption to be noted down [by his secretary] exactly as he observed them." Meanwhile, the younger Pliny recorded,

on Mt. Vesuvius broad sheets of fire and leaping flames blazed at several points. . . . My uncle tried to allay the

*The Roman scholar Pliny the Elder prepares to sail across the Gulf of Cumae to observe Mt. Vesuvius's eruption up close.*

fears of his companions . . . [who were] in darkness, blacker and denser than any ordinary night, which they relieved by lighting torches. . . . My uncle decided to go down to the shore and investigate on the spot the possibility of any escape by sea, but he found the waves still too wild and dangerous.[1]

Pliny the Elder gave his life for science, for searchers later found his body on a beach near Pompeii. About two thousand of the city's twenty thousand inhabitants also met their doom in the catastrophe.

(The rest had the good sense to leave in the early stages of the eruption.) Meanwhile, Pompeii, along with the nearby town of Herculaneum, was buried beneath a thick layer of volcanic debris, wiped from the Roman map, and entombed for what might have been eternity.

In the 1700s, however, Pompeii was rediscovered. Slowly, as the infant science of archaeology gathered steam, succeeding sections of the city saw sunlight for the first time in nearly two millennia. Today, about two-thirds of Pompeii has been excavated. And it is one of the most popular tourist spots in the world,

*Like so many other artifacts from Pompeii, these decorative columns from one of the city's villas have survived intact.*

attracting nearly 2 million visitors each year. The city is also a treasure trove for archaeologists and historians. The debris that buried Pompeii preserved many of its contents intact, including personal items and in one case even loaves of bread left in an oven when the bakers fled; so scholars have learned a great deal about Roman life from studying the city's remains.

Yet it must be remembered that Pompeii is more than a collection of ancient artifacts. It is also the tomb of the thousands of people who met untimely deaths there on a summer's day long ago and a monument to those who built and maintained it in the years before its demise. One who has experienced these haunting aspects of the city firsthand is Jarrett A. Lobell, who worked as an excavator there between 1995 and 2001. After revisiting Pompeii in 2003, he wrote:

As an excavator I always felt very close to the ancient inhabitants of [the city]. On quiet mornings when I was the first person to walk through the empty streets not yet thronged with thousands of tourists, I could almost feel their presence. In the days I spent here as a visitor . . . I felt them again. Many view Pompeii as a sort of memorial to the thousands who died there on one terrifying August day, but what has always affected me more are the thousands that *lived* there until that day. Like the people I used to work with, they are always there waiting for me.[2]

In a sense, the following pages bring these ghosts of Pompeii back to life so that they may reveal firsthand what their lives were like before nature's fury sealed their fate.

# Chapter 1

# A Brief History of Pompeii

As I sit down to write this guide-book in the year A.D. 78, I cannot help but marvel how popular Pompeii is with tourists. One reason for this is that it is a very old city, which makes it very quaint. In fact, it appears to be one of the oldest cities in Italy, which boasts a good many ancient towns. No one knows exactly who established Pompeii and when, but some stories say that the Oscans, an ancient Italian people, first singled out the site and built a fishing vil-

lage on it. This makes sense because Pompeii was, and remains, an important port town, even though it does not lie directly on the seashore. That shore runs along the nearby Gulf of Cumae, named for the leading town in the region—Cumae—situated several miles northwest of Pompeii. (The region I speak of, of course, is Campania, one of the most fertile and pleasant parts of all Italy, indeed of the whole Mediterranean world.) Pompeii can be thought of as a port because it lies on the northern bank of the Sarnus River, which is navigable by ships and connects to the sea at a point not far west of the city.

## Greeks, Etruscans, and Samnites

Pompeii presumably remained an obscure fishing village until the eighth century B.C., when settlers from Greece arrived in Campania. In that bygone era, they colonized much of southern Italy and built numerous towns across the

---

### ⊛ Quick Fact

For those readers who hail from beyond Italy, the Etruscans were a militarily strong and culturally advanced people who occupied a cluster of city-states situated just north of Rome during the centuries when Rome was a young city. Over time, Rome absorbed the Etruscan cities and their inhabitants.

---

area, including Cumae. They also founded the nearby towns of Neapolis (or Naples) and Herculaneum, both lying slightly northwest of Pompeii; and Stabiae, located a few miles south of Pompeii. Having managed to push out the locals (whether Oscans or others unknown), the Greeks took over the small village of Pompeii. They expanded it into an important post in the trading network that they established among their towns. One legend says they built the first temple in Pompeii, in the sector that became known as the Triangular Forum.

*Along Pompeii's main street, the Via Dell' Abbondanza, merchants and pedestrians go about their daily business.*

*The Samnites were strong, courageous fighters. This fresco shows two Samnite warriors in full battle gear.*

in the region was their establishment of the city of Capua, on Campania's northern rim.

Etruscan influence rapidly declined in the fifth century B.C., however, when the Samnites entered the region. As every schoolboy knows, the Samnites were a tough hill people whose homeland was in the rugged heights of the Apennines, the mountain range that runs north to south through the Italian peninsula. It is significant that the Samnites spoke Oscan, the same tongue belonging to Pompeii's founders in the dim past. In about the year 423 B.C., a small Samnite army took Capua. And about two years later larger forces of Samnites occupied Cumae, Neapolis, Pompeii, and Herculaneum.

The cultural effects of the Samnite, as well as the Greek, occupation are still evident in Pompeii all these centuries later. The Samnites were impressed by the Greek culture they found in Campania and adopted many aspects of it. When they began writing down the Oscan language, for example, they borrowed the Greek alphabet since they had no alphabet of their own. The Samnites also adopted Greek business practices, which later passed down through the generations and are still common in the area. It is also interesting to note that,

During the last century of Greek rule in Pompeii and its environs, the Etruscans made several forays into the area. It is uncertain how long they were in Campania and exactly what they did. But it appears that they captured Pompeii and held it for at least a few years. Perhaps the most significant contribution the Etruscans made thanks to the Samnites, a majority of the older buildings in Pompeii were constructed using the Oscan, rather than the Roman, foot and other Oscan units of measurement.

## Enter the Romans

Eventually, for purposes of mutual protection, the Samnites in Campania organized themselves into a loose federation of cities. This proved a wise step, for in the fourth century B.C. new waves of Samnites began to enter the region. These two groups did not see eye to eye. And the Campanian Samnites felt they needed help. So they appealed to the Romans, whose large city-state lay about a hundred miles to the north. A series of three so-called Samnite Wars ensued in the last decades of the fourth century. In their course, the Romans penetrated deeper and deeper into Campania and ended up fighting all the Samnites, including those who had asked them for aid. In about 310 B.C., Roman troops captured Pompeii and Herculaneum.

From that time on, more or less, Pompeii has been controlled by Rome. That does not mean that it immediately became a Roman town in the cultural sense. For the first couple of centuries following the Samnite Wars, Pompeii was better described as an "ally" of Rome (one expected to do Rome's bidding, of course) than a true Roman city. During these years, Samnite, and to a lesser degree Greek, cultural influences and feelings lingered in Pompeii as well as in Herculaneum. Moreover, the

## Rome vs. the Samnites

The Samnites were a robust, industrious people whose homeland lay among the valleys of the central and southern Apennines. There were originally four large tribes (or cantons) of Samnites, each occupying its own territory. Back in the fourth century B.C., these combined territories, and their populations as well, were perhaps twice as large as those of Rome, then a big but solitary city-state. Since both the Romans and Samnites were ambitious peoples, it was inevitable that they would clash; and they did so in three successive wars (which the Romans still refer to as the Samnite Wars). The first conflict, lasting from 343 to 341 B.C., was brief. The Samnites attacked Capua (in Campania), and the town asked the Romans for aid. The latter soon entered and seized control of northern Campania. In the Second Samnite War (326–304 B.C.), invading Samnites captured Neapolis (Naples), prompting the Romans to attack and drive them away. Rome did suffer one notable defeat in this conflict—in 321 B.C. at the Caudine Forks (near Capua). But as they always do, the Romans rebounded and won the war. The last war with the Samnites (298–290 B.C.) witnessed a massive Roman assault on the Samnites' homeland in the Apennines. To their credit, the natives put up a brave defense. However, the outcome—absorption by Rome—was inevitable. The defeated Samnites became Roman allies, and Rome went on to conquer the rest of Italy.

inhabitants still lacked full Roman citizenship and the generous civil rights that come with it.

Pompeii's loyalty as Rome's ally was severely tested on two occasions during these same crucial centuries. The first incident occurred during the Second Punic War (218–201 B.C.), fought between Rome and the great North African trading empire of Carthage. The formidable Carthaginian general Hannibal invaded Italy and inflicted a number of crippling defeats on the Romans. Hannibal realized that he could not completely defeat the Romans and conquer all of Italy unless he gained the support of Rome's many local allies. So he concentrated on winning them over. Capua joined him. But like the majority of the allies, Pompeii and Herculaneum refused. And it

was lucky for them that they did. The Romans soon recaptured Capua, which paid a terrible price for its disloyalty, as its leaders were beheaded and the rest of the citizenry was sold into slavery.

Pompeii passed its first loyalty test, therefore. But it failed its second one. In 91 B.C., 169 years ago to be exact, the so-called Social War erupted. In this conflict, many of the Italian towns that still had the status of Roman ally rebelled because they had long been denied both a voice in Roman government and a share in the wealth gained by Roman conquests. This time, Pompeii, Herculaneum, and nearby Stabiae as well joined the revolt. Not surprisingly, Rome reacted by sending troops to quell the rebels. The noted general Lucius Cornelius Sulla devastated little Stabiae, took Herculaneum, and then laid

*This drawing shows the great Carthaginian general Hannibal (atop the elephant) riding in one of his many victory parades.*

## Capua Is Punished for Disloyalty

After the Romans recaptured Capua, which had joined Hannibal in the Second Punic War, the city paid a heavy price, as related by the first-century B.C. Roman chronicler Livy in his great history of Rome.

All of tho [Capuan leaders] were scourged [whipped] and beheaded. . . . Altogether some seventy loading senators were put to death, and about 300 Campanian aristocrats imprisoned, while others were put under guard . . . and perished in various ways. The rest of the citizens were sold as slaves. . . . All the land and buildings became the public property of the Roman people. The decision was that Capua should remain a city only in the sense of a place of residence; it was to have no political organization, no senate, no people's council, no magistrates. . . . An officer to administer justice would be sent out annually from Rome.

Hannibal

siege to Pompeii, bombarding it with stone artillery balls launched by catapults. (The holes and cracks these missiles made are still visible here and there in the city walls; and a few residents have kept some of the stone balls as souvenirs.)

The Romans won the war. But at its close, in 88 B.C., the Roman Senate saw the wisdom of eliminating the grievances that had caused it. Rome granted all of its Italian allies full citizenship, which meant that Pompeii was at last a true Roman city. In that capacity, eight years later it received an influx of retired veterans from one of Sulla's campaigns in the Near East. They established farms and businesses and their families increased the town's population considerably. There was some friction between these ex-soldiers and the existing residents at first (partly because some of the veterans had taken part in the siege of the city a few years before). But these bad feelings disappeared over time.

## Human-Made and Natural Violence

In the decades that followed, Pompeii prospered. A number of large public structures were erected, including a large stone amphitheater for public games. And the town became famous for its lovely homes and villas and the art treasures housed in them.

Unfortunately, two violent incidents temporarily marred the long period of peace and plenty stretching from the close of the Social War to the present. The first,

*Roman soldiers like these enforced the emperor's closure of Pompeii's amphitheater.*

which took place in A.D. 59, nineteen years ago, was a serious riot in Pompeii's amphitheater. Fistfights, stone throwing, and eventually swordplay broke out between local sports fans and some visitors from the neighboring town of Nuceria (located a few miles east of Pompeii). According to a Roman writer who recorded the incident and its aftermath:

It arose out of a trifling incident at a gladiatorial show given by [a wealthy local man named] Livineius Regulus. . . . During an exchange of taunts . . . abuse led to stone-throwing, and then swords were drawn. The people of Pompeii, where the show was held, came off best. Many wounded and mutilated Nucerians were taken to the capital [Rome]. . . . The emperor [Nero] instructed the Senate to investigate the affair. The Senate passed it to the consuls [two prestigious government officials]. When they reported back, the Senate debarred Pompeii from holding any similar gathering for ten years. Illegal associations in the town were dissolved; and the sponsor of the show and his fellow-instigators of the disorders were exiled.[3]

The other incident was natural in origin, rather than human-made, and caused considerably more loss of life and property damage. It was a violent earthquake. The noted Roman philosopher Seneca the Younger (who died in A.D. 65, during Nero's reign) recorded it for posterity:

*Sulla, pictured here, laid siege to Pompeii in 91 B.C., firing large stone balls into the city.*

I have just heard that Pompeii, the famous city in Campania, has been laid low by an earthquake which also disturbed all the adjacent districts. . . .

It occurred in days of winter, a season which our ancestors used to claim was free from such disasters. [The fourth-century B.C. Greek scholar Aristotle was one of many authorities who said that earthquakes almost always happen in spring and autumn.] This earthquake . . . caused great destruction in Campania, which had never been safe from this danger, but had never been [seriously] damaged [in an earthquake] and time and again had got off with a fright [scary but minor earth tremors]. Also, part of the [neighboring] town of Herculaneum is in ruins and even the structures which are left standing are shaky. . . . Neapolis [Naples] also lost

## Is the Campanian Region Unstable?

In this excerpt from his *Geography*, the Greek scholar Strabo suggests that both the land and sea in the region of Campania is unstable and therefore is unusually prone to earthquakes (and maybe even the fires and destruction associated with volcanoes).

This whole [region], beginning at the Cumaean country [in western Campania] and extending as far [south] as Sicily, is full of fire, and has caverns deep down in the earth that form a single whole, connecting not only with one another but also with the mainland; and therefore, not only [the great Sicilian volcano, Mt.] Aetna clearly has such a character as it is reported by all to have, but also the Lipari Islands, and the districts round about Dicaearchia, Neapolis, and Baiae, and the island of Pithecussae [places in or near Campania]. . . . [Some ancient poets say] that many marvelous things . . . [occurred on] Pithecussae, and that . . . the hill called Epopeus, in the center of the island, on being shaken by earthquakes, cast forth fire and shoved the part between it and the sea back to the open sea; and the part of the land that had been burned to ashes, on being lifted high into the air, crashed down again upon the island like a whirlwind; and the sea retreated . . . but not long after retreating turned back and with its reverse current deluged the island; and consequently, the fire in the island was quenched, but the noise was such that the people on the mainland fled from the coast into Campania.

*The buildings of Pompeii's Forum, mostly rebuilt since the earthquake of A.D. 62, are both imposing and beautiful.*

many private dwellings, but no public buildings. . . . Some villas [in that area] collapsed, others shook here and there without damage.[4]

Unfortunately, much of Pompeii's Forum (main square), in the heart of the town, was badly damaged in the disaster. However, like many other districts, it is speedily being rebuilt by the resilient and industrious Pompeians. Today, therefore, visitors need not worry about a lack of housing or public facilities, as the city is nearly as comfortable and prosperous as it ever was.

## A Bright Future

While still on the subject of the quake of 62, it is worth noting that Seneca also points out some odd occurrences connected with the disturbance:

Certain things are said to have happened peculiar to this Campanian earthquake. . . . A flock of hundreds of sheep was killed in the Pompeian district. There is no reason [that] this happened to these sheep because of fear. For they say that a plague usually occurs after a great earthquake, and this is not surprising. For many death-carrying elements lie hidden in the depths [of the earth]. The very atmosphere there [the area around Pompeii], which is stagnant either from some flaw in the earth or from inactivity and the eternal darkness [under the ground], is harmful to those breathing it. Or when it has been tainted by the poison of the internal fires and is sent out from [deep underground] it stains and pollutes this pure, clear atmosphere [aboveground] and offers new types of disease to those who breath the unfamiliar air.[5]

Some people say that such rancid vapors issuing from the depths and the strange deaths of animals, as well as the earthquake itself, are signs portending some greater future disaster in the region. But as far as this writer is concerned, such ideas are mere rumors that are without foundation and are unduly alarmist. Campania has endured many natural disturbances over the centuries, and Pompeii and Herculaneum have survived them all. So would-be tourists should not let such rumors deter them from visiting these fair cities, which show every indication of enjoying long and bright futures in Rome's great commonwealth.

# Chapter 2

# Physical Setting and Weather

There is no doubt that many of the visitors who make the journey to Pompeii each year are attracted to the area's magnificent setting and climate. Campania in general, but especially the part of Campania surrounding the city, is simply one of the most beautiful places in the known world. In his popular book, published about sixty years ago, the Greek geographer Strabo summed it up this way:

[Campania] is the most blest of all plains, and round about it lie fruitful hills. . . . A proof of the fruitfulness of the country is that it produces the finest grain—I mean the wheat from which groats [a cereal-like product consisting of crushed grains] are made, which is superior, not only to every kind of rice, but also to almost every kind of grain-food. It is reported that, in the course of one year, some of the plains are seeded twice with spelt [another grain], the third time with millet, and others still the fourth time with vegetables. And indeed it is from here that the Romans obtain their best wine. . . . And so, in the same way, all the country round about . . . is well-supplied with the olive.[6]

The olives that Strabo mentions are cultivated in the higher elevations around Pompeii. And the most productive groves rest on the midslopes of Mt. Vesuvius, that picturesque peak that lies only a few miles north of the city's urban area. Also abundant on Vesuvius's slopes

## Travel Tip

Following ancient custom, Pompeii's gates are closed at night and reopen early in the morning. So those taking day trips into the countryside should plan accordingly and make sure to be back inside the city by sundown.

are grapevines by the thousands, each bursting with succulent fruit, the source of Pompeii's famous sweet wine. Lower down, in the meadows, equally numerous herds of sheep graze. They are the basis for one of the Mediterranean's most prosperous local wool operations.

As for the physical look of the city itself, the approaching visitor cannot help but be impressed. This is especially true for those coming from the north, the direction of Cumae and beyond it mighty Rome and its port city of Ostia. As one nears Pompeii from that direction, the first aspect of town that becomes visible is the old defensive wall, which towers to a height of thirty feet in some places. The wall is no longer needed for defensive

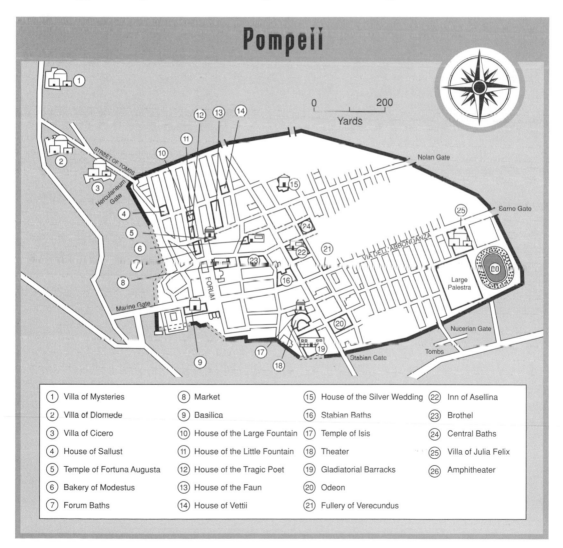

# Pompeii

| | | |
|---|---|---|
| ① Villa of Mysteries | ⑧ Market | ⑮ House of the Silver Wedding |
| ② Villa of Diomede | ⑨ Basilica | ⑯ Stabian Baths |
| ③ Villa of Cicero | ⑩ House of the Large Fountain | ⑰ Temple of Isis |
| ④ House of Sallust | ⑪ House of the Little Fountain | ⑱ Theater |
| ⑤ Temple of Fortuna Augusta | ⑫ House of the Tragic Poet | ⑲ Gladiatorial Barracks |
| ⑥ Bakery of Modestus | ⑬ House of the Faun | ⑳ Odeon |
| ⑦ Forum Baths | ⑭ House of Vettii | ㉑ Fullery of Verecundus |

| |
|---|
| ㉒ Inn of Asellina |
| ㉓ Brothel |
| ㉔ Central Baths |
| ㉕ Villa of Julia Felix |
| ㉖ Amphitheater |

# When Nature Was in a Happy Mood

The noted scholar Pliny the Elder has written about Campania's pleasant setting in his huge tome titled *Natural History*, which he completed last year but has not yet published. The humble author of this travel guide has been privileged to see the work and obtain permission from Pliny to use the following quote.

How am I to describe the coast of Campania, a fertile region so blessed with pleasant scenery that it was manifestly the work of Nature in a happy mood? Then indeed there is that wonderful life-sustaining and healthy atmosphere that lasts all the year through, embracing a climate so mild, plains so fertile, hills so sunny, woodlands so secure, and groves so shady. Campania has a wealth of different kinds of forest, breezes from many mountains, an abundance of corn, vines, and olives, splendid fleeces produced by its sheep, fine-necked bulls, numerous lakes, rich sources of rivers and springs that flow over the whole region. Its many . . . harbors and the bosom of its lands are open to commerce, while even the land eagerly runs out into the sea, as if to assist mankind.

purposes, of course (since Rome controls the whole Mediterranean world and no foreign power would dare attack Italy, the Roman heartland). But its enormous bulk makes tearing it down a task too big and expensive to contemplate!

For entrance into the city proper, look for the Herculaneum, Vesuvius, and Capua gates in the north wall. The Vesuvius Gate affords the most direct and fastest route to the heart of the town. Once inside the gate, you will find yourself on the Via Stabiana, one of the main avenues. Visitors coming from the east should use the Sarnus and Nola gates. The Sarnus Gate leads directly to another principal street, the wide Via Dell' Abbondanza.

Meanwhile, the Nucerian, Stabian, and Marina gates serve the city's southern approaches. Obviously, anyone disembarking from a boat on the Sarnus River will use one of these last three gates.

No matter which gate one uses, a person approaching the city will be struck by how nicely Pompeii fits into its natural environs. Some cities are dirty, dingy, and overall eyesores that mar the natural landscapes that surround them. In contrast, from a distance Pompeii looks fresh, clean, and bright. The white walls and orange roofs of its houses, fringed by the trees and flowers of numerous local gardens, delight the eye and seem an integral part of the lush Campanian countryside.

# A Fortunate and Agreeable Climate

In addition to its special and lovely physical setting, Pompeii enjoys a climate with which few places in the world can compete. Most of the tourists and other visitors who come to the city each year are used to the so-called Mediterranean climate, which features long, hot, dry summers and relatively short, cool, damp winters. Although much of Italy, including Campania, has such a climate, the southern part of Campania, where Pompeii is located, enjoys a particularly fortunate and agreeable version of it. The reason for this is not known precisely. But some people suggest that it has to do with the unique configuration of waterways and landforms in which the city occupies a central position. These include the nearby Gulf of Cumae in the west, lofty Vesuvius in the north, and the Apennine foothills in the east.

Whatever it is that produces the local weather, neither the residents nor visitors

*Tombs line the paved road outside one of Pompeii's gates. Following Roman custom, burials take place outside the city walls.*

can complain. Temperatures average between seventy-seven and eighty-eight degrees (Fahrenheit) in the summer, a season in which it almost never rains. In the fall, temperatures average ten to twenty degrees cooler, but rarely go below sixty degrees. The autumn months are also the rainy season in southern Campania. This is when the locals get the most use out of their cisterns (basins, often located on rooftops, for catching rainwater).

There is less rain in the winter months (January and February), in which the temperature averages about fifty to fifty-five degrees. Keep in mind that it is not unusual to have several sixty-degree days during the short winter. So visitors need not bring along extra warm outfits, as are needed in

*These slaves, who are carrying an aristocrat on a litter, wear tunics, the most common outdoor clothing in southern Italy.*

central and northern Italy during these months. Ordinary tunics will do, although it is prudent to have a shawl or cape to throw over one's tunic in the evenings, when it can get a little cooler. Togas are comfortable in the Pompeian winter. But be warned that the toga is hot and decidedly *un*comfortable in the local summer. (Still, because the toga is so ingrained in Roman tradition as the standard formal outfit for men, it is not unusual to see some Pompeians wearing it even on the hottest days!)

## Quick Fact

Pompeii's outer defensive wall is constructed of large, rough-hewn blocks of limestone and volcanic rock. These form a shell inside of which the builders poured large amounts of earth and rubble, giving the wall tremendous bulk and strength.

# Chapter 3

# Transportation and Lodging

Getting to Pompeii is fairly easy for most travelers. This is partly because the town lies near the sea, making it highly accessible by boat. Pompeii also lies within a nexus of major Roman roads that penetrate or surround Campania, so those headed for the city by land have the benefit of several paved, well-maintained, and safe routes. Travelers can avail themselves of many inns and taverns that lie along the main roads and of course within the city itself. (Indeed, Pompeii is famous for its taverns!)

## Getting There

One's choice of sea or land travel to reach Pompeii depends on a number of factors. First, it is generally more expensive to go by ship. On the other hand, sea travel is a good deal faster than land travel. This is particularly true for visitors who hail from beyond Italy. Those who live in Greece, Egypt, Palestine, North Africa, and Spain, for example, will certainly want to take a ship, as walking will be too time-consuming and exhausting.

Whether your starting point is a foreign land or an Italian port, your ship will eventually enter the picturesque Gulf of Cumae. Here, the view is dominated by Mt. Vesuvius, which can be seen from points all around the gulf. Your vessel will cruise these pleasant waters until it reaches the Sarnus River, south of the mountain. Pompeii's docks lie less than a mile upriver. From the docks, a ramp and stairway lead up a steep grade to the town's Marina Gate. Porters are almost always available to carry one's belongings up the hill, for a fee of course, but the cost is minimal and

## Travel Tip

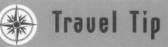

Despite the great distances involved, some people who lack the money for sea passage or who detest riding on ships do end up going by land, even from faraway lands. When possible, utilize carts or wagons, even if only to carry your belongings. Mules, which are also commonly employed to carry baggage, are highly recommended as well.

sonably short trip, depending on one's starting point. People coming from the provinces or foreign lands should take the main trunk roads that lead to Italy. From Spain, Gaul,[7] and other western locales, take the Via Domitia, which runs eastward along the Mediterranean coast and eventually enters northern Italy. If one starts out in Greece, Asia Minor,[8] or other eastern lands, take the roads that connect with the Via Postumia at Aquileia, located on the northern coast of the Adriatic Sea. This will get you into Italy.

Having made it into Italy (or if your starting point is in central or northern Italy), take one of the many main roads that lead to Rome. Then get onto the Via Appia (or Appian Way), which has the distinction of being Rome's first major paved road. It leads southward and winds some 130 miles to Capua, on Campania's

well worth it unless you are traveling light.

Those who choose to go by land will also be greeted by a vista in which Mt. Vesuvius is the most prominent sight. But that is only when they enter Campania itself. Getting to Campania in the first place can be either a very long or a rea-

*This Roman mosaic shows ship traffic on a busy river that flows past a villa. Many people travel to Campania and Pompeii by boat.*

# The Roads of Italy

Augusta Praetoria

Segusio

Mediolanum

Verona ⑥
Mantua ①

Placentia
Dertona
⑥
Cremona

Genua

Aquileia

① Ravenna

Ariminum

Luna
Pisae
Florentia

Vada Volaterrana

⑧

CORSICA

Fanum Fortunae

Arretium

⑪ ④ ⑬ Truentum

Reate

Aternum

*Adriatic Sea*

Tibur ⑦
ROME
Anagnia

Corfinium

② ⑤ Fregellae
Cales
Tarracina

Beneventum

Canusium

⑩

Casilinum
Neapolis Capua
Pompeii

Venusia ②

Brundisium

Tarentum

⑫

SARDINIA

⑨

*Tyrrhenian Sea*

Rhegium

SICILY

① Via Aemilia (187 B.C.)     ⑧ Via Julia Augusta
② Via Appia (312 – 244 B.C.) ⑨ Via Domitiana
③ Via Aurelia                ⑩ Via Trajana
④ Via Flaminia (220 B.C.)    ⑪ Via Cassia
⑤ Via Latina                 ⑫ Via Popillia
⑥ Via Postumia (148 B.C.)    ⑬ Via Salaria
⑦ Via Valeria

0 _____ 100
Miles

northern rim. A bit farther inland from the Appia, the Via Latina also runs southward. It connects with the Appia a few miles north of Capua.

Now, from Rome or other places along Italy's populous western coast, the fastest way to Pompeii is to get off the Appia and onto the Via Domitiana, which continues southward along the coast (while the Appia turns southeastward toward Capua). The Domitiana eventually reaches Neapolis. And from there, a smaller local road

# Many Well-Maintained Roads

Those who were born or raised in the Roman Empire, especially in Italy, the ancient Roman heartland, often take the road system for granted. In contrast, visitors from foreign countries are usually astonished and delighted at the great numbers, lengths, and quality of Rome's roads. Indeed, there is no doubt that the roads of other lands pale in comparison to those in the Empire. Rome has more than three hundred at least partially paved major highways, which together total nearly fifty thousand miles in length. In addition, many thousands of smaller roads branch outward from these main roads, so that overall the road system covers hundreds of thousands of miles. Just as important, the government makes sure that the roads are well maintained. In Italy, this responsibility falls on a special board of curators, with each curator in charge of upkeep on one major road. In the provinces, the governors appoint people from the various towns to take care of the stretches of road that pass through their respective regions.

takes you to Pompeii, just fourteen miles farther south. On the other hand, travelers coming from the inland region or more western locales should stay on the Appia until it reaches Capua. From that town, the Via Campania runs southwestward and connects with the Domitiana at Cumae. (Or you can take one of several unpaved roads that lead more directly to Pompeii from Capua; but be warned that these are not as well equipped and maintained as the main roads and should be avoided in the rainy season, when they become very muddy.)

The use of the word *equipped* above refers to the many important features and conveniences one finds on Rome's principal paved thoroughfares. Added to the sheer numbers of Roman roads and the overall quality of their construction, these amenities are what set Roman roads apart from those in other parts of the world. For example, Rome's major roads are cambered (curved so that the middle is slightly higher than the sides) to make rainwater drain away from the surface. Another helpful feature in some roads consists of artificial ruts carved into the surface to guide the wheels of carts and chariots. These are most effective in stretches of road that are particularly steep or prone to being slippery. Equally helpful are the high, flat-topped stones one finds every few hundred feet or so along the roadsides. Their purpose is to allow travelers riding horses or donkeys to mount these animals easier. Still another useful feature are the milestones (*miliaria*) set on the sides of Roman roads at intervals of a mile. These tell travelers the distances between towns and cities along the road.

## Inns and Other Roadside Facilities

Depending on where one's journey to Pompeii begins, it can take as little as a few days and as long as several weeks. So nearly all travelers who set out for the city must concern themselves with finding nightly accommodations and other kinds of facilities along the roads. In some cases, all that one needs is some water, extra food, or a spare wagon wheel; or you might just want to catch up on the latest news from the capital. To take care of such minor needs, the major roads feature many posting stations (*mutationes*). The government created these primarily to provide fresh horses and supplies to its couriers, who carry messages for the emperor and other officials. But it has become customary for the posting stations to serve everyday travelers as well.

It is important to stress that these posting stations are not equipped with sleeping facilities. To accommodate this need, there are inns (*mansiones*) along the main roads, usually at intervals of between twenty and thirty miles. Their names are often colorful or quaint. Some are named after animals (for example, the Serpents, the Cock, the Camel, the Little Eagle, the Elephant). Others bear the names of gods (the Mercury and Apollo, the Diana), and still others are named after weapons, tools, and other everyday objects (the Sword, the Wheel).

No matter what they are called, roadside inns all offer the same basic services—food, lodging for the night, and a change of wagons or pack animals. And, of course, they also offer plentiful wine to slake your thirst, and, for those men who are interested, female companionship. All of these things are often advertised in pictures and inscriptions painted or carved on an outside wall. One of this writer's favorite inns, located in Aesernia (in the hill country about 120 miles north of Pompeii), has an elaborate sign showing the innkeeper (a woman) settling the bill with a departing guest. The accompanying inscription reads:

"Innkeeper, my bill please!"

"You had one pint of wine, one *as* [a common Roman coin] worth of bread, [and] two *asses* worth of relishes [fruits, vegetables, and other items eaten with bread].

"That's right."

"You had a girl for eight *asses*."

"Yes, that's right."

"And two *asses* worth of hay for your mule."

"That damn mule will ruin me yet."[9]

*One of Pompeii's dozens of inns, seen early in the morning before most people are up and about.*

One thing these inns do not offer is variety, as they all look about the same and have similar layouts. Typically, they are two-story buildings roughly seventy feet long and forty feet wide. Almost always there is a space for wagons and carriages located on one side as well as a stable for travelers' animals. The average roadside inn also provides a blacksmith's forge, a large kitchen, a dining room, and several bedrooms on the second story.

Those travelers who find such inns too impersonal or perhaps desire more privacy can sometimes find lodgings in private houses located near the main roads. The owners rent out rooms, which are usually cheaper and are always quieter and more private than the ones at the inns. In most cases, homeowners who rent rooms hang out signs or plaques to advertise. Most of these bear phrases that are fairly short and straightforward, such as "Rooms Available" or "Travelers Welcome." But a few are longer, more clever, and even memorable. One reads, "If you're clean and neat, then there's a house ready and waiting for you. If you're dirty—well, I'm ashamed to say it, but you're welcome too."[10]

*A drawing shows a well-to-do home on a road near Pompeii. The owner often rents rooms to travelers for a reasonable fee.*

*Figure 1. This painting of the Pompeian magistrate Terentius Neo (brother of local baker Terentius Proculus) and his wife rests in Neo's house.*

*Figure 2. Animal fighters known as "hunters" fight with and kill wild animals in Pompeii's crowded amphitheater.*

*Figure 3. This painting shows men capturing beasts for use in the animal shows presented in the amphitheater.*

*Figure 4. In this section of the "Alexander mosaic" in the House of the Faun, King Darius (on the chariot) flees from Alexander.*

Figure 5. The courtyard
of the House of the
Vettii, a wealthy home
featuring many fine
paintings and mosaics.

Figure 6. Customers buy
fresh loaves of bread at
one of Pompeii's
numerous bakeries.

*Figure 7. The cookshop near the Mercury Fountain is one of the many thermopolii that line Pompeii's main streets.*

*Figure 8. The splendor in which the richest residents of Pompeii live is illustrated by this scene from the House of Marcus Lucretius.*

*Figure 9. Many of the paintings in Pompeii's houses and villas feature a combination of architectural and mythological themes.*

*Figure 10. This decorated fountain, its surfaces lined with seashells, lies in the courtyard of Pompeii's House of the Little Fountain.*

*Figure 11. In this scene from a gladiatorial fight at Pompeii, a retiarius uses his trident to jab at his opponent as a referee looks on.*

Figure 12. The "rape of Cassandra fresco," one of the finest paintings in Pompeii, is located in the House of Menander.

Figure 13. The balcony of a second-story apartment overhangs a sidewalk in the city of Herculaneum.

*Figure 14. The atrium of the House of the Tragic Poet, with its pool for capturing rainwater falling from the open space above.*

*Figure 15. Examples of finely made Roman glass. A few artisans in Pompeii make such items, but most of the glass sold here is imported.*

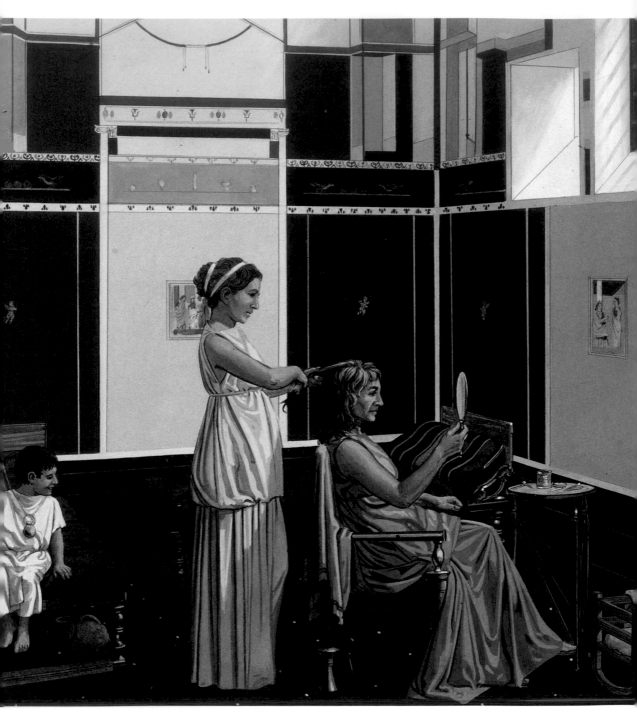

*Figure 16. Members of the family of L. Ceius Secundus in a domestic scene in one of the bedrooms of his Pompeian home.*

*Figure 17. The counter of a snack bar faces directly onto the sidewalk. For a small fee, such establishments will cook food brought by patrons.*

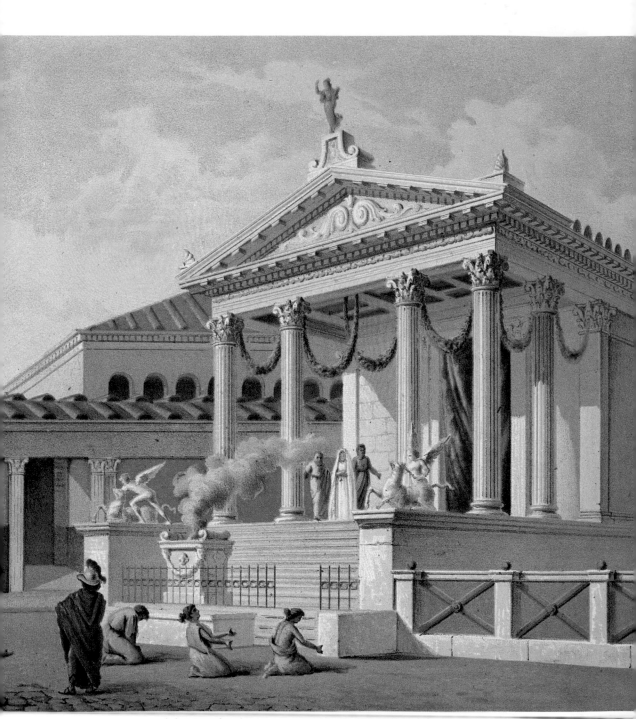

*Figure 18. A view of the Temple of Fortuna Augustus, on the edge of the Pompeian Forum. Note the sacrificial fire on the altar.*

## The Inns of Pompeii

Travelers headed for Pompeii (or anywhere else for that matter) are not always forced simply to take their chances in choosing a place to stay for the night. People who like to plan ahead can avail themselves of maps and guidebooks (called itineraries) that are available in most cities. The itineraries list the towns, inns, stables, major sites, and other notable places along one or more major roads. Most of the maps and itineraries feature little numbers indicating the distances between towns, inns, and other stopping places. And some of the more expensive versions also include little picture symbols that rate the quality of these facilities. For instance, a picture of a four-sided building with a courtyard in the middle indicates an inn with superior facilities, while a symbol that looks like a house with a twin-peaked roof indicates a country inn of only average quality.

Once the traveler has made it to Pompeii (in one piece, it is hoped!), he or she will find many inns and hotels. But keep in mind that the crowded conditions that are a fact of life in all cities dictate that most of these facilities are smaller than the av-

*A wall inscription from Pompeii.*

crage roadside inns. The guest rooms in the city inns are generally smaller, too, and a good many have no windows. In such situations some managers supply the guests with candles or oil lamps. But some do not, so the smart traveler is the one who carries his or her own candles or oil lamp.

C·GAVIVM·RVFVM  II VIR
OF
VTILEM·R·P·VESONIVS·PRIMVS·ROGAT

## Ancient Pompeii

This is not to say that the hotels in Pompeii are all cramped and dark. A few are fairly spacious and quite elegant. There is the House of Sallust, for example, located in the western part of the city near the junction of the Via Consolare and Mercury Lane. When it was first built a few centuries ago, it was a well-to-do private home. Like many such early Pompeian mansions, however, during the city's first-century B.C. expansion phase, the house was slowly but steadily converted into a more commercialized property. Small shops and snack bars were added to the front facade on the ground level. And some of the bedrooms on the

*The interior of the famous House of Sallust, which was built as a private home, but now features guest rooms and restaurants.*

second story became hotel guest rooms. Today the House of Sallust is particularly noted for its small but excellent restaurants, one of which features tables on an outdoor terrace.

Most of the hotels in town are smaller, consisting of a few guest rooms located above or in back of a tavern. One of the most popular is Asellina's Tavern (sometimes called Asellina's Inn), situated right on the Via Dell' Abbondanza (Pompeii's main commercial street) in the center of the town. Asellina, a woman and one of the friendliest innkeepers in the city, is assisted by some equally sociable (and quite pretty) waitresses and female bartenders—Smyrna, Maria, and Aegle. Like a number of other Pompeian taverns, the place specializes in wine heated in kettles.

Visitors should be aware that a majority of the smaller inns and hotels lack in-house plumbing facilities. So if your budget demands staying at a cheaper place with no running water and no toilets, you might want to plan accordingly. A number of inns are located near public fountains (where most people get their drinking water) and toilets (in which the wastes are efficiently eliminated through pipes or troughs by streams of running water). Having such facilities close at hand is convenient, but at least ask your host if he or she supplies chamber pots in case of an emergency. If not, we advise buying one so as to avoid the unfortunate experience of one poor fellow who left the following message on a wall outside his hotel: "Dear host, I'm afraid I've wet the bed. 'Why?' you ask? because there was no chamber pot in my room."[11]

# Chapter 4

# Restaurants and Food

When the traveler is satisfied that he or she has found decent lodgings in Pompeii, the next step is usually to locate the nearest and best places to eat. On this score, visitors are in luck, as Pompeii has many fine eating establishments, which range from fancy sit-down restaurants, to snack bars offering fast food, to cozy bars and taverns. Lumping all of these eateries together, the city has well over 150 in all, more than enough to accommodate locals and visitors alike. Of course, every one of these places has its regular customers, especially at traditional meal-

times, and therefore the places can sometimes be crowded. So for those travelers who prefer solitude, there is also the option of going to the market, buying your food, and eating alone in your room.

## Finer Restaurants

Let us begin with formal restaurants (*popinae*). These generally feature one or more small dining rooms equipped with tables and chairs. (The main dining room in an average Pompeian *popina* measures roughly seven by fifteen feet, while smaller rooms are about seven feet square.) The nicest restaurants have one or more private rooms with couches around the tables for those who prefer to recline, rather than sit, while eating. They also provide bathrooms with plumbing similar to the kind seen in the public toilets. Some *popinae* furnish entertainment as well, including musicians, dancing girls, and occasionally jugglers and other specialty acts.

**Travel Tip**

Visitors who are renting rooms in local houses can sometimes work out kitchen privileges for a reasonable fee, an ideal arrangement.

This elegant private dining room features couches for guests to recline on while eating. Slaves do most of the serving.

# Entertainment in Eating and Drinking Places

The entertainment at Pompeian eateries and bars can be both varied and enjoyable. The nicer places feature soft, soothing music, usually someone playing the lyre (a small harp) and singing traditional melodies of the countryside. Some of the taverns, on the other hand, offer more spirited music and a few have female dancers. Prostitutes are available at most taverns or inns; one needs only to ask the manager or bartender. And, of course, plenty of gambling, one of the most popular leisure activities in the Empire, goes on in the local taverns. Dice games are especially popular. One Pompeian tavern has some funny scenes, complete with captions, painted on the inside walls. Of these, a memorable one shows two gamblers arguing. "Strike me dead!" one says. "I swear to you that I won!" The other fellow curses at him and adds, "No, *I* won!" The next drawing shows the proprietor tossing them out into the street and telling them to do their fighting there.

The most popular restaurants of all (although also the most expensive) are the ones that offer outdoor eating areas. These have awnings to shade the guests on hot days and usually feature handsome manicured gardens to please the eye and nose. In addition to the one at the House of Sallust, a smaller but admirable outdoor dining area can be found at an eatery just north of there, right near the Herculaneum Gate. Much bigger is the open-air facility at the *popina* near the amphitheater on the other side of town. The tables in this lovely restaurant are intertwined among the hanging vines of a grape arbor some sixty feet long and thirty feet wide. Needless to say, we recommend this one highly, although you should expect to wait a while to be seated at suppertime.

## Cookshops and Taverns

For faster, simpler fare, Pompeii has close to 140 *thermopolii* (small cookshops or snack bars) and taverns (see Figure 7). You can find them all over the city; but the largest concentrations are along the busy Via Dell' Abbondanza; near the city's gates (to attract hungry travelers just arriving); and around the amphitheater and theaters. Actually, there are few city blocks that do not have at least one cookshop or tavern, and some have several.

The difference between these two kinds of eatery is not all that great and some can be classified as both a cookshop *and* a tavern. Basically, a cookshop features a marble- or slate-topped counter opening onto the sidewalk. Customers walk up to the counter and order,

after which they can either stand there and eat or take the food back to their rooms. The cooking is done on a metal grill over a small charcoal furnace recessed into the counter (see Figure 17). Recently cooked food, such as sausages and other grilled meats, is kept warm in ceramic jars stacked nearby. Cold items, including bread, cheese, figs, dates, nuts, and cakes, are common fare at such snack bars.

One of the more popular cookshops is that of Vetutius Placidus, located on the Via Dell' Abbondanza very near the large House of Amaratus. The very friendly Vetutius Placidus lives in a small house connected to his eatery, so it is rare not to see him serving food from behind his three-sided counter. Visible behind the counter, toward the back of the shop, is his personal shrine, of which he is quite proud. In addition to clay figurines representing his household gods, there are small statues of Mercury (god of profit as well as protector of travelers) and Bacchus (god of wine).

In contrast, a tavern is usually a little larger than a cookshop and features at least a few tables and chairs for the customers. Also, though one can buy wine at a *thermopolium*, the variety and quality is generally limited; whereas the average tavern has a larger variety of wines to choose from and can offer some of the better imported wines.

# Wine Lovers Take Notice

This is a good place to digress for a moment and talk about the wines available in Pompeii and, for the sake of foreigners, the manner in which Romans drink their wine. First, the tavern keepers obviously want to bring in as much money as they can; so they often make it a point to advertise that they do carry some of the finer, more expensive wines. The outside wall of one local tavern, for instance, bears a painting showing a waitress pouring wine for a customer, accompanied by the caption, "A cup of Setian, too!"[12] This, of course, refers to the fine wine produced at Setia, located in the hill country north of Campania.

Another Pompeian tavern (which is also an inn) has a sign reading, "For one *as*, you can get a drink here. For two *asses*, you will get a better drink. For four *asses*, you will drink Falernian wine."[13] Falernian, which the Roman poet Horace frequently praises in his writings, is widely seen as the finest wine in Italy.

One of the more crucial considerations for tavern keepers and their customers alike is the mixing of wine. Following ancient custom, almost all Romans mix their wine with water in a large bowl called a crater, after which they pour or ladle it into goblets. A person who drinks undiluted wine is generally

*Patrons must be wary of unscrupulous tavernkeepers who add too much water to their wine.*

considered a rube or a peasant (in some places even uncivilized!).

As for the ratio of wine to water, it differs from place to place and is sometimes a matter of personal taste. Most commonly, Romans prefer to use more water with heavier, sweeter wines and less water with lighter, drier wines. One thing is certain. Some tavern keepers and innkeepers, including a few in Pompeii, have been known to add extra water in an effort to make the wine go further and cheat the customer. Complaints are not uncommon. But a particularly notable one was lodged not long ago by an angry customer, who went out and wrote on a tavern's wall: "May you soon, you swindling tavern-keeper, feel the anger divine, you who sell people water and yourself drink pure wine."[14]

Assuming one's wine is not overly diluted, there are other ways to mix it besides using only water. Some visitors (as well as a number of the locals) prefer their wine sweetened with honey. Romans call this popular wine "punch" *mulsum*. Various spices are commonly thrown in, too. You can get one or another version of *mulsum* at virtually every bar and catery in Pompeii. Keep in mind that local Pompeian wines tend to be quite sweet already (something to do with the unusually rich soil in the area), so one can feel safe ordering them without honey and spices.

## Catering to Roman Tastes

Whether they be formal restaurants, cookshops, or taverns, all such establishments in Pompeii serve foods of various kinds as well as wine. In general, Pompeian eateries cater to Roman tastes (since most of the tourists who visit the city each year are from other parts of the Empire). So the following section about common Roman foods and mealtimes is included for the benefit of foreign visitors who may be used to different foods and meal schedules.

For Romans, breakfast is most often a light meal. The most common breakfast foods are bread or wheat biscuits, which people dip in wine or smear with honey. It is not unusual to have a little cheese or some olives or raisins along with the bread. Visitors from places like Germany, where it is customary to eat some form of meat along with bread at breakfast, will find plenty of meat available at most cookshops in the city. (Pork is the favorite meat of Romans, but several kinds of fowl, along with lamb, venison, and fish, can be had, too.)

*A carved scene shows the proprietor of a cookshop serving a young man. Nearly all cookshops serve pork.*

Many Romans eat a light lunch in the early afternoon. This meal usually consists of cold foods such as bread, salads, and fruits. It is a fairly common sight to see people of all walks of life having their lunch on street corners or in open areas like the Forum on nice days. Again, for those who prefer a hot meal, one is nearly always available from a *thermopolium* (except late at night).

In most parts of Italy, as well as in some of the provinces, the main meal of the day is taken either in the late afternoon or early evening. Depending on what a person can afford, or on personal preference, supper can be either simple or elaborate. In Pompeii's finer restaurants, such as the one at the House of Sallust, supper is usually served in three courses, collectively called *ab ovo usque ad malla* ("from the egg to the apples"). In the first course, diners enjoy appetizers, including eggs, raw vegetables, mushrooms, oysters, and/or sardines. Next comes the second and main course, consisting of cooked meats and

*Pompeii's finer restaurants use expensive silver dinnerware.*

vegetables. The third course is the dessert. Fruit, nuts, and/or honey cakes and other pastries are the usual fare.

For visitors who prefer more exotic foods, especially imports from distant provinces and countries, some are available periodically in Pompeii's marketplace. But their availability varies widely. This is because shopkeepers and food sellers are dependent on whatever foreign items arrive on merchant ships. And these vessels do not always carry the same foodstuffs. Assuming one does find such items, cooking them does not present a problem for those visitors who have no immediate access to kitchens. Most cookshops will heat up whatever you give them for a small fee.

## The Pompeian Bakers

No discussion of available foods in Pompeii would be complete without mentioning the city's many bakeries. There are nearly forty of them in all, and they constitute one of the most vital and integral aspects of local economic and gastronomic (food-related) life. This is because a majority of Pompeians and visitors do not bake their own bread, one of the world's staple foods. Instead, local farmers sell the bulk of the grain they grow directly to *pistores*, who are combination miller-bakers, with their shops in town. The bakers use big millstones to crush the grain. Then

## Preparing a Popular Dessert

Here are the ingredients and the instructions for combining them for a dessert that is very popular in Pompeii and other Roman cities—egg pudding.

Serves 4. 3 eggs, 3 tbs. flour, 1¾ cups milk, pepper to taste, 2½ oz. pine nuts, 1–2 tbs. raisin wine, 4 tsp. honey. Beat the eggs in a bowl with the flour and milk. Add pepper and heat in a pan. Meanwhile, grind the pine nuts with the raisin wine in a mortar. As soon as the egg mixture begins to boil, remove from the heat. Add the honey and the pine nut mixture. Resume cooking for approximately 15 minutes more over a low

heat, stirring so that no lumps form. Pour into 1 large or 4 small individual bowls; add a teaspoon of honey and a pinch of pepper to each and serve.

they convert it into dough and bake it in brick ovens, which are mostly heated by charcoal.

For those foreigners who have never had the privilege of seeing a Roman bakery in action, this guidebook recommends visiting the one owned and run by Modestus. It is located on a little side street not far south of the Via Dell' Fortuna, on the city's west end. Modestus is happy to allow those who are interested watch him and his bakers (mostly slaves and freedmen) turn out their loaves and other products.

There are at least eight other bakeries within a few blocks of Modestus's shop. So it is not surprising that that district is known for its wonderful, mouth-watering aromas, not to mention its mountains of fresh and delicious breads and pastries. Each baker has his specialty, so it cannot hurt to check out as many of these shops as time allows so as not to miss out on some really memorable baked goods. (As an added boon, if you have a pet dog, some of the local bakers make dog biscuits that are so tasty that some people have been known to buy them for themselves!)

# Chapter 5

# Bathing and Exercise Facilities

After lodging and food, the central personal concern of most of the people who visit Pompeii (especially Romans and Greeks) is finding proper bathing and exercise facilities. Fortunately for them, the town is well en-

*This room in Pompeii's Forum Baths houses one of the cold pools (presently drained during repairs).*

dowed with both. In fact, the first public bathhouses (*thermae*) at Pompeii and nearby Herculaneum were the prototypes for the larger versions that later sprang up in Rome and larger cities. (Pompeii has always been a trendsetter; its amphitheater, which will be described in a later chapter, was the first all-stone version in the Roman realm.) Another first for Pompeii was the twenty-foot-wide dome above the cold room in the city's Stabian Baths. This was the earliest complete dome constructed in a public building in Italy.

## Available Facilities and Their Hours

In all, Pompeii has four public bathhouses. These are the Stabian Baths, conveniently located at the junction of the Via Dell' Abbondanza and Via

*This cutaway drawing shows the layout of the Stabian Baths as seen from the east.*

Stabiana (which gave these baths their name); the Forum Baths, situated on the Via Dell' Fortuna, a short distance northwest of the Forum; the Central Baths, at the junction of the Via Stabiana and Via Dell' Fortuna; and the Amphitheater Baths, just off the Via Dell' Abbondanza, near the amphitheater.

As a matter of fact, accessibility is a chief concern for all who contemplate attending the baths. Be aware that the hours of these facilities can vary. But they generally open around one or two in the afternoon, signaled by the sound of a bell or the loud announcement of a slave. All are open well into the night, during which they are well lit by large numbers of oil lamps, which the slave-

attendants refill on a regular basis. The Forum Baths and Stabian Baths have separate facilities for men and women. (Mixed bathing, a bit more common in the highly urbanized Rome, is frowned on here.) The other bathhouses in Pompeii stagger their hours to accommodate male and female bathers.

## ✳ Travel Tips

Please note that the Stabian Baths were badly damaged in the quake of 62 and parts of the building are still under repair. So it presently offers only limited facilities, and before entering one should check with the manager about which sections are open.[15] The Central Baths, a new facility, is also under construction, but it is scheduled to open soon. Watch for announcements on the city walls.[16]

# Private Bathhouses

In addition to the large public bathhouses in Pompeii, there are a few smaller private ones. One of the nicest is the Venus Baths, run by the well-to-do matron Julia Felix. Her large house was badly damaged in the quake of 62, and to help offset the cost of repairs she installed these baths, which she rents out to people interested in running a bath business. In fact, she is presently advertising for a new manager:

> For Rent: from August 13, with a 5-year lease on the property of Julia Felix, daughter of Spurius [Felix], the elegant Venus Baths, streetfront shops and booths, and second-story apartments.

*Toilette articles*

Regarding exercise facilities, Pompeii features a large *palaestra* (sports center), which is located right alongside the amphitheater on the eastern edge of town. There is also a smaller *palaestra* in the southern part of Pompeii, next to the theaters and the Temple of Isis. In these places you can jog, play handball or *harpastum* (a ball game featuring teams of players), lift weights, wrestle, box, throw the discus, do gymnastics, or practice fancy horsemanship (assuming you have brought your horse along with you). It should be noted that most of the people who frequent the large sports center are from the working classes. A majority of well-to-do Pompeians usually patronize the smaller center or attend the still smaller (but well-equipped) *palaestrae* offered in the public bathhouses. (The Stabian Baths have small but exceptionally pleasant exercise and ball-playing areas, for example.)

Indeed, the big public bathhouses in Pompeii are not just for bathing. They offer many other leisure and social services and opportunities. For example, all four establishments are busy social centers, where people converse with friends and exchange the latest news and gossip. On the other hand, some patrons mix business with pleasure by meeting with business associates, clients, or patrons at the baths.

One can find even more to do than bathe, exercise, and socialize at the public bathhouses. Some of these places have small restaurants or snack bars catering to bathers or sports enthusiasts who have worked up an appetite. Others offer gardens and reading rooms. The specific "extra" features offered by each establishment vary, but all have the same basic kinds of reception and bathing rooms.

## From Hot to Cold to Hot to Cold

These rooms follow a general pattern familiar to all patrons of Roman bathhouses.

First, one enters the lobby, which doubles as a reception room. (Some of the much larger bathhouses in Rome have separate meeting rooms, some of them quite spacious.) From the lobby, the patron enters the locker room (*apodyterium*), undresses, and leaves his or her clothes with a slave for safekeeping.

What happens next depends on the person, as each bather has his or her preferred

*A scene from the women's facility in the Stabian Baths. Mixed bathing in these baths is strictly prohibited.*

routine. However, the most common order followed is to go from the locker room to the *tepidarium*, a warm room without a bath. There, the patron sits for a while until he or she begins to sweat. Then comes the *frigidarium*, a room with one or more pools of cold water, which are meant to refresh the body after its initial sweat. (Of course, some people prefer to plunge right into the cold water without working up a sweat first.) After exiting the cold pool, the patron generally dries off with a woolen towel.

After the cold room, most people go to the hot room (*caldarium*), which features one or more pools of steaming hot water. It is advisable to linger there and enjoy the feeling of the heat opening your pores. Foreigners who do not have the benefit of such facilities in their native lands often ask how this heat is produced. Local bathers enjoy explaining to them that the device in question is fairly simple and straightforward—hot air generated by a fire circulates in hollow spaces under the floor and inside the walls.

When one has had enough of the hot room, he or she can either enter the sauna (*laconicum*) or take another dip in the *frigidarium*. Whichever option is chosen,

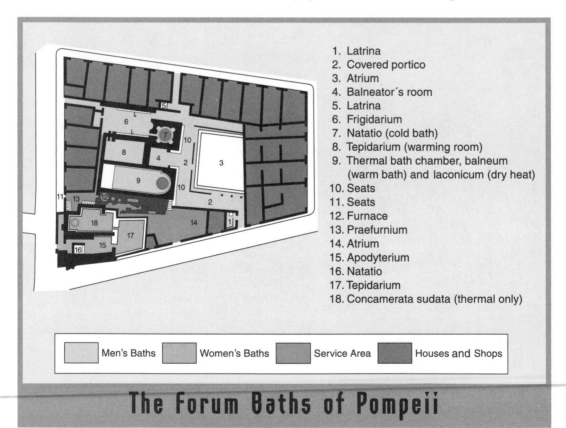

1. Latrina
2. Covered portico
3. Atrium
4. Balneator´s room
5. Latrina
6. Frigidarium
7. Natatio (cold bath)
8. Tepidarium (warming room)
9. Thermal bath chamber, balneum (warm bath) and laconicum (dry heat)
10. Seats
11. Seats
12. Furnace
13. Praefurnium
14. Atrium
15. Apodyterium
16. Natatio
17. Tepidarium
18. Concamerata sudata (thermal only)

Men's Baths     Women's Baths     Service Area     Houses and Shops

## The Forum Baths of Pompeii

## ✦ Bathhouses Can Be Noisy

The exercise rooms and swimming pools of the larger bathhouses can be quite noisy places. One is reminded of the humorous anecdote cited by the noted playwright Seneca the Younger in one of his published letters in which he complains about the noise from the bathhouse below his apartment:

> For someone who wants seclusion to read and study . . . I'm really in trouble. . . . Just imagine the whole range of voices which can irritate my ears. When the more muscular types are exercising and swinging about lead weights in their

A pair of women's bath slippers (left); an oil flask and some strigils (above).

hands, and when they are straining themselves, or at least pretending to strain, I hear groans. And when they hold their breath for a while and then let it out, I hear hissing and very hoarse gasps. . . . Now, if a ballplayer comes along and begins to count his score aloud, I'm definitely finished. . . . And then imagine people diving into the pool with a great splash of water.

many patrons eventually continue on to the *unctorium*, or "oil room." Here, you can rub oil (olive oil is the most popular kind) on your body and scrape it off, along with any dirt and sweat, with a strigil (a wooden or metal scraper). As is the case with towels, you should bring your own oil flask.[17] One can also get a massage (from a bathhouse slave) in the *unctorium*, which is always a popular service.

It is clear by now that some bathers enjoy going back and forth from the hot

## Quick Fact

Foreigners take note: Clients and patrons are members of the common Roman institution of patronage. Less-well-off clients are socially and often financially dependent on their well-to-do patrons and are expected to do favors for them on a regular basis; this can include meeting a patron at whatever time and place is convenient for him or her.

pools to the cold ones more than once in a single visit. Some patrons stay for hours and make this circuit several times. Others show up only to use the swimming pool (*natatio*), as swimming is an excellent form of exercise that both tires and relaxes a person very quickly. Still others linger in one room or another because they enjoy the atmosphere and decorations, which can be quite luxurious. The cold room in the Stabian Baths, for instance, is particularly stunning. Its ceiling and walls are lined with magnificent frescoes (paintings done on wet plaster), including scenes of gardens, fountains, and doves drinking from said fountains. This and other excellent amenities make the Stabian Baths a highly recommended destination for all who visit Pompeii.

# Chapter 6

# Exchanging Money and Shopping

Visitors will find a multitude of shops of every conceivable kind in Pompeii. They are scattered all around the city. However, the largest concentrations of them are found in two places—the Forum, which bisects the Via Dell' Abbondanza in the west end, and along the Via Dell' Abbondanza itself. In these areas you will find food vendors, bakeries, fabric shops, wool sellers and fullers (fabric dyers and clothes cleaners), glass and jewelry shops, potters, metalsmiths, leather sellers, woodworkers, and many more.

It should be emphasized that Pompeii is more of a resort town than a manufacturing center. As a result, few local products are widely sold beyond Campania. Pompeian *garum* (fish sauce) and wine are two of a few notable exceptions. On the other

hand, to keep up with the needs and desires of its residents, as well as the travelers and tourists who come here, Pompeii imports goods, especially luxury goods, from far and wide. So it is not unusual to find Pompeian shops selling sturdy furniture made in Capua and Neapolis, finely crafted terra-cotta (baked clay) figurines from the island of Pithecussae; oil lamps from northern Italy; pottery from Gaul; olive oil from Spain; wine from Spain, Sicily, and Crete; and carpets from Egypt and other parts of the Near East.

Another thing worthy of note about Pompeian shops are the shopkeepers themselves. They are a hardworking and proud lot who demand and deserve respect. Often the trades and shops in the city are family businesses in which everyone in the family pitches in to help. It is

*Customers stop at the shop of the bronzesmith Verus. Like most other local artisans, he makes his wares on the premises.*

not unusual, for instance, to see a male potter or fuller working in the back room with his sons and slaves while his wife or daughter deals with the customers in the front room that lines the street.

Although these tradespeople routinely compete in the marketplace, outside of the business realm they are very supportive of one another. As in other parts of the Empire, they have guilds (*collegia*), in many cases one for each trade. These are essentially social organizations in which people of like skills, professions, backgrounds, and interests get together outside of work. Members of the guilds elect officers to run their meetings. (This is one of the few ways that poor and uneducated people can experience leadership roles in the community.) And they pay annual dues. The money is used to finance guild religious festivals and to pay for the burials of guild members.

Considering how closely knit the local merchants are, the visitor is strongly advised to stay on their good side. If you steal from one shop and try to hawk the item at another, the proprietor of the second shop will likely report you to the authorities. Another way that shopkeepers track down stolen items is by offering rewards. Only recently a local coppersmith posted the following notice outside his establishment: "A copper pot is missing from this shop. I offer a reward of 65 *sesterces* for its return, and a reward of 20 *sesterces* for information leading to its return."[18]

## Coins and Exchanging Money

This shopowner's mention of the *sestertius*, a common Roman coin, leads us into the important topics of money and currency exchange, which the visitor needs to address before he or she actually begins shopping in Pompeii. Residents of the Empire are already familiar with the coinage. But foreigners need to know that the basis of the realm's coinage is the *aureus*, a gold coin equal in value to ¹⁄₄₀ of a pound of gold. The other standard coins are the *denarius* (worth ¹⁄₂₅ of an *aureus*), the *sestertius* (worth ¼ of a *denarius*, or ¹⁄₁₀₀ of an *aureus*), and the *as* (worth ¼ of a *sestertius*). Occasionally the visitor will deal with pocket change, including the *quadrans* (or penny, worth ¼ of an *as*). Those travelers who are carrying non-Roman currencies (such as Syrian or Persian), bronze ingots, jewelry, or other valuable items will need to exchange them for more acceptable Roman coins.

## Guild Support for Local Leaders

Even a quick glance at the walls of Pompeii will reveal the fact that the workers and their guilds are very interested in local politics. The following election ads show their support for one local official or another:

The fullers ask you to elect Holconius Priscus as *duovir* [one of two administrators in charge of running the town].

All the carpenters ask you to elect Cuspius Panza as aedile [an official in charge of maintaining the streets and public buildings].

The fruit sellers ask you to elect Marcus Holconius Priscus as aedile.

The barbers want Trebius as aedile.

The chicken sellers ask you to elect Epidius and Suettius as *duovirs*.

The innkeepers urge you: "Make Sullistius Capito aedile."

*Local bankers will exchange coins like this one for gems and other valuables.*

To exchange your currency or valuables or to borrow some money to live on while waiting for funds to arrive from home, the visitor needs to go to a local banker (*argentarius*). Pompeian bankers are private businessmen who charge a fee or earn interest for dealing with people's financial needs on an individual basis. (Most of them come from humble backgrounds and several are former slaves. This is mainly because members of the upper classes tend to feel that dealing directly with money is beneath their dignity.)

The bankers have tables set up in various sectors of Pompeii, but not surprisingly most are found in the main shopping districts. Whichever banker you choose will carefully weigh all coins and other valuables for a fee based on a percentage of the amount of money exchanged. The standard rate at the mo-

ment is about 6 percent. Many bankers will also loan money (at rates of 6 to 10 percent); take money and other valuables on deposit (so you do not have to carry around a large, heavy bag of coins and risk losing it); and buy, sell, and manage real estate (land and buildings).

Most of the Pompeian bankers are reputable. But the most experienced and almost certainly the most successful (and richest) one in town is Lucius Caecilius Jucundus. He has a large, well-furnished home on the Via Stabiana, just north of the junction with the Via Dell' Fortuna. But he is seen more often in the shopping districts, especially in the main market in the Forum. To show prospective new customers how reputable he is, he has allowed two transactions from his older account books to be published here. One reads:

Umbricia Januaria declares that she has received from Lucius Caecilius Jucundus 11,039 *sesterces* which sum came into the hands of Lucius Caecilius Jucundus by agreement as the proceeds of an auction sale for Umbricia Januaria, the commission due him having been deducted. Done at Pompeii, on the 12th of December [A.D. 56]. [The signatures of several witnesses are included to attest that the transaction was honest and fair.]

Another reads:

On the 18th of June [A.D. 59] . . . I, Privatus, slave of the colony of Pompeii, declared in writing that I had received from Lucius Caecilius Jucundus 1,675 *sesterces*, and previous to this day, on June 6, I received 1,000 *sesterces* as rent for the public pasture. Done at Pompeii. [Several witness signatures are appended here, too.][19]

## The Pompeian Fullers

When the visitor has concluded his or her business (if any) with a banker, it is time to begin shopping. In the Forum marketplace, as well as in some smaller shopping areas in various sectors of the city, vendors set up their wagons, tents, or other temporary stalls in the open spaces. Many of them pack these up at night and unpack them the next morning. However, Pompeii has hundreds more permanent shops constructed of stone or brick (or both). These shops often identify themselves by little signs painted on the outer walls facing the street; typically, such renderings show one or more of the main items sold inside. The shopkeepers also frequently hang or stack some of their merchandise on outward-facing counters or racks or even right on the sidewalk.

Such merchandise takes many forms. Among the most common merchants in Pompeii are bakers, fullers, and *garum* sellers. Since bakers have already been

## Snooty Attitudes About Work and Money

The reason that bankers, shopkeepers, and other tradespeople are almost never rich aristocrats is plain. The latter view everyday work activities, especially those dealing directly with exchanges of money, as beneath their dignity. In his treatise *On Duties*, the famous first-century B.C. Roman orator and senator Marcus Tullius Cicero summed up this rather snooty attitude this way:

As for crafts and other means of livelihood . . . [those] that incur the dislike of other men are not approved, for example, collecting harbor dues, or usury [moneylending]. Again, all those workers who are paid for their [manual] labor and not for their skill have servile and demeaning employment; for in their case the very wage [they receive] is a contract to servitude. Those who buy from merchants and sell again immediately should also be thought of as demeaning themselves. For they would make no profit unless they told sufficient lies, and nothing is more dishonorable than falsehood. All handcraftsmen are engaged in a demeaning trade; for there can be nothing well bred about the workshop. The crafts that are least worthy of approval are those that minister to the pleasures, [including] fishmongers, butchers, cooks . . . fishermen . . . perfumers, dancers, and the whole variety show [theatrical acts and displays].

described, let us consider the fullers, whose industry is the most important in town. (There are as many as forty fulleries in Pompeii, more than in most other towns of similar size.) Fullers have two basic jobs—to refine and convert raw and rough woolen material into acceptable fabrics and to clean existing fabrics. One of the leading fullers in Pompeii is a freedman named Stephanus, who has a big shop on the Via Dell' Abbondanza, two blocks east of the junction of the Via Stabiana. He is highly recommended, although many other local fullers are very skilled and reliable.

One of these other fullers, Lucius Veranius Hypsaeus, had some artists paint pictures of various stages of the fuller's trade on the walls of his own establishment. As these show, the cloth is first cleaned and thickened. This is done partly by immersing it in a large vat filled with "fuller's earth," an absorbent clay mixed with potash and urine. (The urine comes not only from the fullers and their assistants but also from customers and passersby, who are encouraged to pee into pottery jars hung on the fullery's walls; when a jar is full, the fuller's assistant replaces it with an empty one.) The fullers work the cloth into the fuller's earth, either by kneading it with their hands or by trampling it with their feet. Then they rinse the pieces of cloth in vats of clear water and hang them on clotheslines to dry in the sun.

*Several open shops are visible in this Pompeian street scene.*

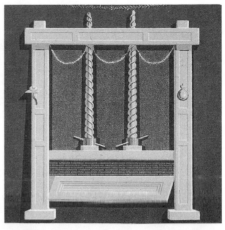

*These pictures show dyeing, pressing, drying, and other aspects of the fuller's trade.*

The last stage in the fulling process is the dyeing of the cloth. This is accomplished by placing it in a kettle of boiling water and adding the desired colored dye. (The dyes come from various minerals or vegetable extracts.) Vinegar is often added to make the colors adhere better to the cloth. Finally, the cloth is heated in a stove, and when it comes out it is attractive and soft, yet durable.

Some fullers sell the finished cloth in big or small rolls directly to the public. But just as often they sell it to merchants who transform the cloth into clothes items and sell them. Of course, large numbers of Pompeians and other Romans buy the fulled cloth and make their own clothes.

## From Fish Sauce to Gladiator's Blood

Many other products can be bought in Pompeii besides cloth and clothes, of course. Of these, the local *garum*, an unusually tasty fish sauce, is in high demand

73

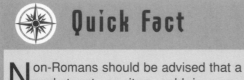

## Quick Fact

Non-Romans should be advised that a pocket set, an item sold in many Pompeian shops, is a small leather pouch containing tweezers, a nail cleaner, an ear cleaner, a toothpick, a small mirror, and some basic makeup items.

throughout large parts of the Empire. Because Pompeii lies near the sea, it has a prosperous fishing industry. And the locals not only sell and eat a lot of fish, they also turn a considerable portion of each catch into *garum*. The king, so to speak, of the Pompeian fish sauce vendors was the late Marcus Umbricius Scaurus, whose tomb can be seen near the Herculaneum gate. He grew quite rich from his trade and sometimes used his wealth to finance gladiatorial shows in the city's arena.

*Garum* sellers like Scaurus make their famous product in the following manner. First they chop up pieces of fish and fish eggs. To this they add the guts of sardines and then pound the mixture (with wooden hammers), stir it thoroughly, and leave it in vats out in the sun. After about six weeks, the mixture ferments. At this point, it

is poured into a basket with little holes punched in the bottom. The liquid that seeps out through the holes and into storage jars is the highly prized *garum*. (To the surprise, and often squeamish stomach, of many non-Romans, the mushy leftovers are considered edible, too. Called *allec*, this pungent fish product is sold separately in all of Pompeii's fish and *garum* shops.)

Many visitors will no doubt want to purchase a jar of local *garum* as a gift to take back home to family and friends. But many other items sold in Pompeii make suitable gifts and souvenirs. These include grooming items such as hairbrushes, tweezers, skin creams (many made from olive oil

*An aristocrat uses stepping-stones to avoid puddles and garbage while crossing the street.*

mixed with various other substances), and perfumes. Standard "pocket sets," always very popular with the ladies, are available, of course, in a number of local shops.

Other popular gifts sold in Pompeian shops include jewelry (rings, earrings, brooches, gold chains, bracelets, anklets, medallions, cameos, and so forth); fine glass-ware (much of it from Rome and even some from the Near East) (see Figure 15); well-made leather shoes and boots; swords and other weapons; butcher knives; cooking pots and tableware; pottery vases, pitchers, and drinking cups; and metal figurines (many depicting popular gods and goddesses).

Among the most popular of all the souvenirs bought in Pompeii are those related to gladiators. In large part this is be-cause people come from many of the sur-rounding towns to enjoy the combats held periodically in the local amphi-theater. Used swords, helmets, greaves (metal lower-leg protectors), and numerous other items from the arena are big sellers. So is so-called gladiator's blood, which many people be-lieve will cure various physical ailments. Whether or not there is any truth to this, visi-tors who are contemplating buying some are warned to be careful. There is no way for the customer to tell if the blood in the vial he or she purchases actually came from a gladiator; often, sheep's or pig's blood is sold to the unwary and gullible. For the most part, Pompeian merchants are honest. But there are always excep-tions to every rule.

# Chapter 7

# The Amphitheater and Public Games

Travelers come to Pompeii for a wide variety of reasons, ranging from business to pleasure. On the pleasure side, some visitors are gladiator enthusiasts, as each year the Pompeian arena attracts people from as far away as Rome in the north and Brundisium in the south. A major reason for the popularity of these local games is that Campania, perhaps the area of Pompeii itself, was the place where Roman gladiators and their sport originated.

The proof for this, the experts say, are old tomb paintings in the region, dating

*Tomb paintings from Paestum, south of Pompeii, show warriors grappling in ancient funeral games, the origins of gladiatorial fights.*

elaborate athletic contests and other public displays in his honor. These included chariot races, boxing matches, and, in Campania, armed combats between warriors armed with swords and spears. The Paestum paintings show such armed pairs, along with referees who regulated their matches.

These were the first gladiators, although they were not yet called by that name. Also, their fights were not yet meant as public entertainment; rather, the blood they spilled and lives they lost were intended to honor the person who was the object of the funeral. Only much later, after these contests spread to other regions, especially Rome, did the citizenry start to demand that they be made public.

Another piece of evidence showing that Campania was the home of the first gladiators comes from the pen of the great Livy. He points out that the most common general gladiator type—the Samnite—originated in Campania way back during the Samnite Wars, when the Samnites occupied Pompeii and the region surrounding it. After defeating them, Livy says, the Romans staged a big triumph (victory parade) to show off the prisoners and weapons they had captured:

*The armor and weapons of a typical Samnite gladiator are familiar to all Romans.*

from as early as the fourth century B.C., almost five hundred years ago. A series of particularly colorful and detailed ones at Paestum, located just a few miles south of Pompeii, show scenes from ancient funeral games. In those days, when a general or other important man died, people held

By far the greatest sight in the procession was the captured armor, and so magnificent were the pieces considered that the gilded shields were distributed amongst the owners of the silversmiths' shops to adorn the Forum [Rome's main town square]. . . . While the Romans made use of this armor to honor the gods, the Campanians, out of contempt and hatred towards the Samnites, made the gladiators who performed at their banquets wear it, and they then called them "Samnites."[20]

## The First Amphitheaters

Still more proof linking the region of Pompeii to the earliest gladiatorial bouts are the facts that the first and most important gladiator schools were built in Campania (including the ones at Capua and Pompeii) and that the first all-stone amphitheaters were erected there. In fact, Pompeii boasts the first one in the entire Empire! This alone makes the town a very historic site and a popular tourist spot.

Before describing the Pompeian amphitheater and telling about the games presented in it, it will be helpful to give some information on how this structure and others like it came about in the first place. These unique buildings, which the Romans invented and perfected, evolved gradually from smaller, less durable, and less impressive structures. In fact, if one delves back far enough in time, he or she will find that there were once no formal arenas at all. Back then, gladiatorial fights were held only occasionally. And when they were, they took place in wide, open areas, most often town forums. As the late and highly respected Roman architect and engineer Marcus Vitruvius Pollio said in his important book *On Architecture*, "The custom of giving gladiatorial shows

## Some Amphitheaters Are Unsafe

The Pompeian amphitheater was erected partly to allay local fears that the traditional portable wooden versions were sometimes unsafe. This worry was borne out in A.D. 27, half a century ago, when the wooden amphitheater built at Fidenae, a town located north of Rome, collapsed. According to one account:

An ex-slave called Atilius started building an amphitheater at Fidenae for a gladiatorial show. But he neither rested its foundations on solid ground nor fastened the wooden superstructure securely. He had undertaken the project not because of great wealth or municipal ambition but for sordid profits. Lovers of such displays . . . flocked in—men and women of all ages. Their numbers, swollen by the town's proximity, intensified the tragedy. The packed structure collapsed, subsiding both inwards and outwards and . . . overwhelming a huge crowd of spectators and bystanders. Those killed at the outset of the catastrophe at least escaped torture. . . . More pitiable were those, mangled but not yet dead, who knew their wives and children lay there too. In daytime they could see them, and at night they heard their screams and moans. . . . Fifty thousand people were mutilated or crushed in the disaster.

*On a day when games are presented in the Pompeian amphitheater, spectators shop in an open market on their way inside.*

in the forum has been handed down from our ancestors."[21]

Over time, the crowds for these displays got bigger and bigger. So it seemed prudent to erect special structures to accommodate them. The first amphitheaters were made of wood and were portable—meaning that they were pieced together, dismantled, and later assembled again as the need for them arose. Some were left standing for several seasons before being dismantled.

It is interesting to note that, though they were impermanent, these early amphitheaters were sometimes very large and lavishly decorated. They required immense quantities of wood and nails (as well as numerous laborers) to build, so not surprisingly they were very expensive and only wealthy people could afford to erect them. Most of the architects and builders of these structures were skilled and reputable. But on occasion poor design and shoddy materials were used. This could be dangerous for the spectators, as in the case of one such wooden amphitheater that collapsed during the middle of a show back in A.D. 27, killing large numbers of people.

## The Pompeian Amphitheater

Long before this disaster, however, the people of Pompeii saw the wisdom of building a safe and permanent facility for gladiatorial games. The Pompeian amphitheater was completed in 80 B.C. The names of the two far-sighted public officials who financed and oversaw its construction—Quinctius Valgus and Marcius Porcius—can still be seen in the dedicatory inscription. These generous men did a great service to their fellow citizens as well as to all future generations of Pompeians; namely, they donated the structure and the land on which it sits to the town for all times.

Another thing to be noted in the dedicatory inscription is that it does not call the structure an amphitheater. This is because the term *amphitheatrum* had not yet been coined! Instead, people then called the building, along with any of the wooden versions still being built, a *spectaculum*, meaning a "place for spectacles." It is obvious that the builders had some reasonably large-scale spectacles in mind because the place is huge—easily the largest structure in the city (indeed, in the whole region). It is essentially a big oval bowl measuring 445 by 341 feet. And it can accommodate up to twenty thousand people, nearly the entire population of Pompeii. The arena floor, where the combats are held, is sunken below the level of the outside ground. In this arrangement, a massive earthen embankment helps support the great weight of many of the rising tiers of stone seats. Meanwhile, a series of high brick arches on the outer perimeter provides support for the building's curved walls and exterior staircases.

Those visitors who attend games at the Pompeian amphitheater for the first time are always impressed by the numerous comforts and amenities the facility provides. These include elegant decorations, such as statues on pedestals, tapestries hanging on walls; cushions for the spectators to sit on; and snack bars surrounding the complex. (Of course, some people prefer to bring their own food from home.)

Perhaps the most important amenity offered at the amphitheater is the huge awning (*velarium*) that shades the audience on hot, sunny days. Without it, spectators would become overheated as well as develop painful sunburns! Indeed, the awning is so crucial to putting on a good and comfortable show that it is frequently mentioned in the ads for the games seen on the city's walls. One recent ad reads, "The gladiatorial troop hired by Aulus Suettius Certus will fight in Pompeii on May 31. There will also be a wild animal hunt. The awnings will be used."[22] A longer and much more colorful ad of this type was done by Aemilius Celer, one of the leading sign painters in Pompeii and a very clever fellow:

Twenty pairs of gladiators sponsored by Decimus Lucretius Satirus Valens, lifetime priest of Nero Caesar [part of the local cult that worships the emperor as a semidivine being], and ten pairs of gladiators sponsored by Decimus Lucretius Valens, his son, will fight in Pompeii on April 8, 9, 10, 11, and 12. There will also be a suitable wild animal hunt. The awnings will be used. Aemilius Celer wrote this, all alone, in the moonlight.[23]

## The Gladiators and Their Local Barracks

Some visitors to Pompeii, especially those who have never seen gladiatorial games before, ask if the gladiators live and train somewhere within the amphitheater itself. The answer to this query is no. The fighters have their own separate barracks (or school), located on the southern edge of town just south of the theater district.

(The placement of the barracks there, away from houses, streets, and most people, is no accident. As is well known, gladiators are popular when they are fighting one another in the arena; but socially speaking, they are considered lowlifes, and city officials do not want them mixing with and offending the sensibilities of the citizenry.)

Another often-asked question is: Who are these persons who are so popular as warriors but so detested as people, and why would they choose such a profession? The truth is that only a small percentage of the gladiators who fight here actually choose the profession. The vast majority of gladiators in Pompeii and elsewhere are prisoners, slaves, and criminals who are forced into it. As for the few people who actually volunteer, some do so because they are experiencing financial troubles

*Despite their low social status, gladiators are popular with young women, as shown in this scene from a fight staged in a private home.*

and simply need the money. (Prize money is usually provided for the winners of the matches.) Others volunteer because they find such dangerous combat a challenge.

And still other volunteer fighters want to take advantage of the fact that gladiators are often sex symbols who attract pretty young girls (or boys, as the case may be). This aspect of the gladiatorial life can be seen in several inscriptions on the city's walls. One reads, "Caladus, the Thracian, makes all the girls sigh." And another says, "Crescens, the net fighter, holds the hearts of all the girls."[24] (These "girls" are most often members of the poorer classes, as it is viewed as socially unacceptable for well-to-do young women to make public displays of any kind, much less fuss over disreputable characters like gladiators.)

Whatever the reasons may be that individuals become gladiators, they all end up enduring the same strict and punishing regimen at the training barracks. Indeed, even the trainees' living quarters in the Pompeian barracks are designed to toughen them both physically and mentally. These quarters consist of rows of

cell-like cubicles—some on the ground level, the others above them on a second story—all lining the square-shaped central exercise grounds. Each cubicle is about twelve feet across and most of them have no windows or skylights. Neither do they have furniture, with the exception of crude wood-framed cots on which the inmates sleep.

Outside of these cold and grim living quarters, the only other indoor areas the trainees are allowed in are the kitchen and prison. The kitchen is a big room with a huge hearth on which slaves cook the gladiators' food. The inmates sit at tables set up nearby and are closely guarded as they eat. The prison has a ceiling so low that a person locked inside cannot stand up and must spend all of his time either sitting or lying down. In addition, prisoners are shackled in large, painful leg irons and are given very little to eat. Clearly, the manager of the barracks wants any rule breakers who are sent to this dungeon to find it so unpleasant that they will commit no further infractions.

One place the inmates are never allowed to enter is the barracks armory. They never have access to weapons when they are away from the training grounds, and with good reason. First, an inmate might use a weapon to kill himself and thereby end his servitude (assuming he is not one of the volunteers). In such cases, the manager might receive

*This bas-relief carved from terracotta shows arena fighters sparring with a lion in one of the popular beast shows.*

a fine, or even be fired, for allowing the destruction of valuable property; after all, most of the trainees are slaves in whose upkeep the government has invested a good deal of money.

Even worse, inmates who get hold of weapons might use them against the trainers or guards in an attempt to escape. Thanks to the precautions and vigilance of the manager and guards, escapes from gladiator barracks are extremely rare. But when they do occur they can be very troublesome, even frightening, especially if a group, rather than an individual, escapes. No one wants a repeat performance of the infamous Spartacus incident, which happened right here in Campania. For those few who may not know that name, back in the 70s B.C. he led a mass escape of slave-trainees from a

gladiator barracks in Capua and terrorized people in the surrounding countryside for months before the government sent troops to crush him. For a while, the escaped slaves had a camp on the slopes of Mt. Vesuvius, only a few miles from Pompeii. (If you have a morbid fascination for such things, for a fee a local guide will take you up to see the spot.)

Getting back to the gladiators' strict training regimen, the recruits have to perform incessant drills, partly to toughen their bodies and partly to learn to fight and kill with precision. To these ends, the instructors (*doctores*) watch the trainees' footwork, lunges, and parries closely and correct any mistakes immediately. The trainees also do drills in which they attack a stationary six-foot-tall wooden pole (*palus*) with a wooden sword (*rudis*) or spear. Such exercises are meant to develop better reflexes and hand-to-eye coordination, which are crucial to winning matches later in the arena. The whole time that these drills are going on, dozens of armed guards stand on the perimeter of the training grounds, ready to capture or kill any inmate who might attempt to escape.

## The Arena Battles

Eventually, new recruits become well-trained fighters and graduate to their first bouts in Pompeii's amphitheater. On the day of a scheduled show there, the gladiators first enter the arena in a festive parade (*pompa*). It is quite a show, as they are accompanied by musicians playing marching music and by acrobats, jesters, and other entertainers who cavort around to the audience's delight. After these entertainers make their exit, the gladiators draw lots to decide who will fight whom, and an official inspects their weapons to make sure they are sound and well sharpened. Finally, the fighters raise their weapons toward the highest-ranking official present and in unison say the words, "We who are about to die salute you!" Then it is time for the first match.

The kinds of gladiators one will see in the opening fights vary from show to show. There are certainly plenty of gladiator types from which to choose. Most Romans are ardent games fans, so they are very familiar with these types, but for the sake of foreign visitors who have never seen gladiators in action, a brief description follows.

The Samnite gladiator has already been mentioned as the first recognizable type that evolved. He gave rise to others who are armed in a fairly similar manner, among them the *secutor*, *myrmillo*, and *hoplomachus*. All of these types wear metal helmets, protective armor on one or both arms and legs, and carry large shields. The traditional Samnite, along with the *secutor* and *myrmillo*, wields a sword almost identical to the thrusting sword used by Roman soldiers. The *hoplomachus*, by con-

*A company of gladiators enters the arena during the* pompa.

trast, carries a spear. (The other differences are minor. For example, the *secutor*'s helmet is more rounded than that of a traditional Samnite and has smaller eyeholes; and the *myrmillo*'s helmet has a distinctive fish crest on it.)

A completely different sort of gladiator, the *retiarius* wears little or no armor and carries a net, with which he tries to ensnare his opponent. If he is successful in this maneuver, the *retiarius* stabs the fellow with his other weapon—a long, razor-sharp trident (three-pronged spear) (see Figure 11). Other gladiator types include the *equites*, who fight on horseback using lances, swords, and/or lassoes; the *essedarii*, who battle from chariots; the *dimachaerii*, who fight with two swords (or daggers), one in each hand; and the *andabatae*, who go at each other while blindfolded by big helmets having no eyeholes!

The combats in which these and other gladiator types engage are usually fast paced and exciting. And some, as expected, end with the death of one of the fighters. However, a fair number of some matches end in a draw, in which case both men walk away and face the prospect of fighting in future games. Another common outcome is when one gladiator is wounded and falls to the ground. He is allowed to raise one finger, signaling an appeal for mercy. At that point, the local magistrate in charge of the games (or a higher official who might be visiting Pompeii) makes the decision either to let the wounded fellow live or to condemn him to death. If it is the latter,

## Retired Gladiators in Pompeii

Working gladiators are almost never seen on Pompeii's streets since they are considered social misfits or dangers to the community, or both. However, from time to time one might see a retired gladiator shopping or otherwise going about his business. They are usually called *rudiarii* (a name that comes from the *rudis*, the wooden sword they originally trained with and which is given to them as a ceremonial gift after their final matches). Most of these arena veterans are presently working as instructors in the city's gladiator barracks. Because they are not much more socially accepted than working gladiators, they tend to keep to themselves and their own kind and maintain a low profile. However, they could not have made it to their retirement if they had not been top-notch fighters. So they often remain popular with hard-core arena fans, who periodically call for the veterans to make brief comebacks. Some *rudiari* are fairly well-to-do thanks to the large sums of money paid to them for these comebacks. For instance, the emperor Tiberius (who reigned from A.D. 14 to 37) paid some retired veterans a thousand gold pieces each (the equivalent of many years' salary for the average person) to appear in a single match.

the victor slits the loser's throat without further ado. (In some cases, the magistrate checks with the crowd first; and if most of the spectators want the downed fighter to be either spared or slain, he will usually go along with them.)

## Wild Beasts and Trained Animals

The Pompeian amphitheater does feature other shows besides gladiatorial bouts, of course. The principal alternative arena attraction consists of the wild animal shows, which are guaranteed to delight locals and visitors alike. These shows pit people against beasts and beasts against other beasts. They are generally called hunts, although this name is a little misleading. The "hunters" are trained killers—essentially lower-level gladiators—who do not stalk their prey in the wild but rather slaughter them in the confined space of the arena. Still, such fights are often fraught with danger and elicit loud reactions from audiences. (Some spectators actually root for the animals!)

The beasts one will see in these shows come from all corners of the known world. They include lions, tigers, leopards, bulls, crocodiles, bears, elephants, and ostriches, among others. In some cases, they fight to the death with a hunter (*venator*), who brandishes a spear, a sword, a club, a bow and arrow, or some other weapon. In other cases, attendants chain two animals together and goad them to attack each other.

Not all of the animals in these shows are killed, however. It is not unusual to see tame and delightful trained-animal acts, in which the beasts perform all manner of tricks. For example, monkeys dressed as soldiers are seen driving miniature chariots drawn by goats. And this author has witnessed a lion hold a rabbit in its jaws without injuring the smaller creature! Still other examples are bears trained to play ball and elephants that dance and drink from cups in an amazingly civilized manner!

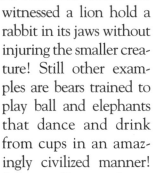

Whether it be a gladiatorial bout, a charging bull, or a trained elephant, every show presented at Pompeii's renowned arena is worth seeing. And attending that facility is always highly recommended for anyone visiting the city.

# Chapter 8

# Things to See and Do in Pompeii

The public games are a major attraction for tourists and other visitors to Pompeii. But they are far from the only things of interest to see in the city. As pointed out earlier, Pompeii is an ancient town with a considerable mixture of old and new cultural aspects. These range from impressive public buildings and venerable religious temples to large private houses and villas containing magnificent works of art.

## Learning to Navigate the Streets

Finding one's way to the various sights in town is usually fairly easy because the streets, with a few minor exceptions, are laid out in an efficient grid pattern. Thus, most houses, shops, and public buildings lie within rectangular city blocks. The two main avenues, of course, are the Via Dell' Abbondanza and the Via Stabiana. They intersect at the Stabian Baths, in the south-central part of the city. Just about every other street in town runs off of one of these two or the third major avenue—the Via Dell' Fortuna, which connects with the Via Stabiana at the Central Baths.

Of the city's streets, the Via Dell' Abbondanza is the widest, measuring about twenty-five feet across throughout most of its length. In contrast, most Pompeian streets are much narrower—averaging about eleven feet in width. This narrowness, combined with the existence of many overhanging balconies on the second floors of houses and shops, creates a

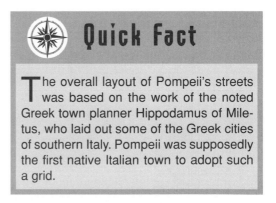

### Quick Fact

The overall layout of Pompeii's streets was based on the work of the noted Greek town planner Hippodamus of Miletus, who laid out some of the Greek cities of southern Italy. Pompeii was supposedly the first native Italian town to adopt such a grid.

considerable amount of shade, which helps pedestrians keep cooler on hot summer days.

As for the construction of the streets, they are made mostly of large slabs of hard, gray rock mined from the base of Mt. Vesuvius. In some places, especially on the main avenues, one will see ruts worn into the pavement by centuries of wagon and chariot traffic. Many side streets lack these ruts because they are closed to such traffic and allow only pedestrians. The main streets also have raised sidewalks and crosswalks with high stepping stones, so that pedestrians do not have to trudge through the garbage and dirty water that often collects in the streets.

## The Old and New Forums

Where these streets will take the visitor depends a great deal on what he or she is interested in seeing. This writer advises starting at the beginning—timewise, that is—and taking a look at the city's oldest public buildings. If you are so disposed, take the Via Dell' Abbondanza to the Stabian Baths and across the way from them turn south and go two blocks. You will come to a low hill topped by the so-called Triangular Forum, the heart of the city in its earliest centuries. (The term *so-called* refers to the fact that it was never a true forum but more of a fortress and religious center.) Here, at least six and possibly seven centuries ago, the Greeks erected

*The Temple of Fortuna Augusta is the local home of the imperial cult, which worships the emperor as semidivine.*

The biggest building in the Forum area, lying on its western edge, is the Basilica, measuring 180 by 90 feet. This is the town's main place for commercial and social meetings. Inside, there is a large, two-story-high central hall, with several small meeting rooms lining its sides.

## The Temples Under Repair

The second-most imposing structure lining the Forum (on its northwestern corner) is the Temple of Jupiter, leader of the gods. Pompeii has numerous temples and

*A columned, covered walkway lining the border of the Forum (left); the Basilica, the largest structure in the Forum (below).*

the city's first temple. It presently lies in a state of ruin, a perpetual reminder of Pompeii's great age. Around it an imposing portico (roofed walkway) with a hundred columns, which was built in the second century B.C., remains in use.

Only a few blocks west of the Triangular Forum is the modern Forum, its open rectangle encompassing an area about 500 feet long and 150 feet wide. Stately colonnades (rows of columns) line three sides of the rectangle and directly behind the columns are a number of imposing buildings. Three are halls for local government business (one for hearing court cases and taking the census, one housing the offices of aediles, and one for meetings of the town council).

## The Temple of Isis

Among the other Pompeian shrines damaged by the quake of 62 was the Temple of Isis, located just northwest of the city's large theater. Isis, of course, was originally an Egyptian goddess of fertility and marriage (and the sister and wife of the god Osiris, whom the Romans often call Serapis). In the last couple of centuries, she has become quite popular across the Roman Empire, and many Roman towns have erected temples in her honor. The rituals and beliefs perpetuated by these shrines include initiation rites, baptism, and the promise of eternal salvation. Pompeian worship of Isis has been influenced and strengthened by a direct connection with Egypt, namely the prosperous trade route between Pompeii and Alexandria (Egypt's capital). Pompeians view Isis as a compassionate mother figure, and she is pictured in local art holding or nursing her son.

shrines, each dedicated to a certain god. (An exception is Jupiter's temple, which also honors Jupiter's wife, Juno, and Minerva, goddess of wisdom, the arts, and war). Unfortunately, the Temple of Jupiter was badly damaged by the quake of 62. But the repairs are going well, and some worship (in the form of animal sacrifices) already takes place at the altars set up on the grounds.

Most of the other temples in Pompeii were also hit hard by the quake. One of these, the Temple of Apollo, located near the western edge of the Forum, is very old and has numerous large statues of the god on the grounds. The tremors knocked these statues down, but some survived almost intact. Long ago Apollo was Pompeii's patron deity (special divine protector), until that honor passed to Venus, goddess of love, for a time. (Today, Jupiter is the city's patron.)

Speaking of Venus, her temple, located on the edge of town southwest of the Forum, was almost completely leveled by the quake. Consequently, the decision was made to demolish the ruins and erect a completely new temple on the spot. So far, the foundation is in and the bases of many of the main columns have been installed. The new building is scheduled for completion in four to five years.[25]

## The Theater District

While most of the temples in town suffered badly in the quake, the two theaters, major local venues for the arts, fortunately came through with only minor damage. The large theater, which rests on the eastern flank of the Triangular Forum, was originally constructed in the Greek style—with a circular orchestra (acting area) at ground level in front of the rising rows of seats. In Sulla's time (early first century B.C.), however, a Roman-style raised stage was added, along with a large wall behind it.

For the most part, full-length plays are presented in this theater. These are mostly Roman versions of older Greek plays, primarily comedies. The two most popular Roman comic playwrights are still the masters Plautus (third century B.C.) and Terence (second century B.C.). Plautus's *Pot of Gold*, about an old miser who fears that somebody will steal his life savings, is a perennial favorite. Tragedies are less popular with Pompeians (and most other Romans) and therefore are presented far less often than comedies in the large theater.

In contrast, tragedies are seen more commonly in the small theater, or Odeon, located right next door to the large theater. The Odeon is used mainly for poetry recitations and musical presentations. But large-scale versions of Seneca's tragedies, including *Medea* and *Phaedra* (both based on the Greek originals), have been presented here as well. (Seneca's tragedies are designed to be read, rather than acted out, by the performers.)

In general, Pompeii's theaters do not draw the kind of crowds the amphitheater does. But they still attract good-size audiences on a regular basis. This is attributable in part to the popularity of some of the local actors as well as some nationally known actors who periodically come to Pompeii to perform. Among these, Lucius Domitius Paris is a big crowd pleaser.

*A procession of musicians highlights a show in the Odeon, Pompeii's smaller theater.*

## Mosaics and Paintings

Other examples of the fine arts in Pompeii consist of the many magnificent mosaics and paintings scattered throughout the town. Some of these are in public buildings. But many of the best ones are in private houses. Those visitors fortunate enough to be invited to dinner in these homes will find the decor more rewarding than the food.

The mosaics are a marvel to behold, for example. These generally adorn floors or walls but are also used to decorate the undersides of arches and ceiling panels. To make them, craftsmen place small stone or glass cubes, tiles, or marbles into wet cement. Some mosaics have abstract themes, for instance repeating geometric patterns or shapes. Others are more realistic and show scenes of temples, houses, landscapes, gods, people, animals, and real or mythical events.

Frequently, the scenes in Pompeii's most splendid mosaics are copied directly from existing paintings, some of them quite old. As a result, such mosaics have managed to preserve the appearance of a number of paintings that no longer exist. Perhaps the most striking example is in the House of the Faun, located on the Via Dell' Fortuna two blocks west of the Via Stabiana. This wonderful mosaic shows the Greek conqueror Alexander the Great attacking the Persian king Darius III during the Battle of Issus (which took place in 333 B.C.) (see Figure 4). Based on a lost painting by the Greek master Philoxenos of Eretria, the work is composed of at least 1.5 million individual tiny pieces of colored stone and glass.

Although a number of other old paintings have been lost over the years, many high-quality ones have survived and are right here in Pompeii. The best ones are wall murals. Examples with architectural themes often cover entire walls and include life-size representations of columns, furniture, doors, windows, and so forth. In this way, they become an integral part of

*This detail from the "Alexander mosaic" in the House of the Faun shows the Greek conqueror himself, poised to attack his Persian enemy.*

# The House of the Vettii— a Private Art Gallery

Pompeii's House of the Vettii has so many beautiful paintings in it that the locals think of it as the town's foremost private art gallery. A lovely mansion owned by two prosperous merchants—Aulus Vettius Restitutus and Aulus Vettius Conviva—the house is located in the block that faces the inside of the Vesuvius Gate. The first batch of paintings one encounters when entering the place are in the atrium (front hall). Many more artworks can be seen in other rooms and on the walls of various corridors. Among them are many showing cupids (representations of the younger form of Cupid, son of the love goddess, Venus), some riding crabs, dolphins, and other sea creatures, others satirically engaged in wine selling, crafts, and other human activities. The house also has some large painted panels of famous myths, including Dirce being trampled by a bull and Pentheus being torn apart by a group of mad women.

the decor of whatever room they are in. Also very common are painted scenes showing landscapes, incidents from everyday life, and mythological characters. Of the latter, one of the best is a depiction of the baby Hercules fighting with serpents, which is in the House of the Vettii (on the southern edge of the block nearest the Vesuvius Gate) (see Figure 5).

Some of these wall paintings are done on wood panels. But most are frescoes, executed directly on wet plaster. The manner in which this technique is accomplished is as follows. First the artist applies two or three thin layers of lime-stone plaster to the wall. Then he or she paints the background, which frequently shows distant landscapes or nearby buildings. When the plaster and paint have dried, the painter adds human and animal figures and other details. After this stage of the painting has dried well, the artist applies a coating of transparent glue or wax, which creates a bright, glossy, very durable surface. Like so many other artistic and architectural wonders in Pompeii, the paintings are made to last a long time (assuming that nature's fury does not intervene, as it unfortunately did in the quake of 62!).

# Chapter 9

# Day Trips to Nearby Towns and Sights

W hile visiting Pompeii, some visitors take side trips to nearby towns and other sights of interest. The region is certainly rich and diverse in culture and natural resources, and those who do go on such excursions always find them rewarding. For the traveler's convenience, the sights will be arranged according to their distance from Pompeii, beginning with those that are closest to the city and proceeding outward.

## On the Road to Vesuvius

To find the first item of interest beyond Pompeii, one needs only to walk outside

*Leaving the city through one of its many gates, visitors may take short trips to other sites of interest in Campania.*

*This fresco is one of many in Pompeii and sur-rounding towns and villas that art enthusiasts must see when visiting the area.*

the Vesuvius Gate on the northwestern side of the city. There, near the highest point in the town, the local aqueduct enters. It is one of many aqueducts in central Italy and other parts of the Empire that bring freshwater from lakes and mountain streams into populated areas that lack sufficient supplies of that vital resource. This aqueduct begins in the mountains some twenty-five miles east of the coast. At one point it splits into two branches, one heading northward to Neapolis, the other southward to Pompeii. The aqueduct itself is a stone channel that runs underground most of the way. Only when it crosses ravines or low valleys does it appear in the open, carried on top of a series of graceful stone arches called an arcade. One such arcade can be seen in the fields just outside the city.

After the aqueduct, the next point of interest for the visitor is the village of Boscoreale, located a couple of miles north of the town on the bottom slopes of Mt. Vesuvius. It is not a village in the traditional sense (a collection of poor huts and small structures) but rather a group of stately rural estates and mansions. Some of the wealthiest men in the Empire have houses here. And the art treasures in these homes are renowned. One, the Villa Pisanella, boasts one of the world's richest collections of silver objects, including cups, pitchers, bowls, serving platters, and mirrors. Another villa at Boscoreale, the home of Publius Fannius Sinistor, has a magnificent series of colorful wall murals with architectural themes.

Leaving the area of Boscoreale, one encounters the great bulk of Vesuvius itself. The mountain is about twelve miles around at its base and rises to a height of about four thousand feet. The name Vesuvius has a derivation the visitor may find interesting. The mountain has always been sacred to the legendary strongman and hero Hercules (whom the Greeks call

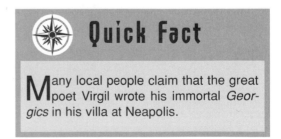

## Quick Fact

Many local people claim that the great poet Virgil wrote his immortal *Georgics* in his villa at Neapolis.

Heracles); and as everyone knows, he was a son of the great god Zeus. Now, one of Zeus's very ancient names was Ves. In Greek, *vesouuios* means "son of Ves," which over time was corrupted into the more familiar "Vesuvius."

## The Paintings in Sinistor's Villa

For those fortunate enough to see the interior, the villa of Publius Fannius Sinistor at Boscoreale (two miles north of Pompeii) is a marvel to behold. Built in about 40 B.C., a little over a century ago, it contains some of the most beautiful paintings in the Roman world. (Most of the paintings date from the 30s B.C.) One small room alone, measuring only twenty-five square feet, features nine large painted panels. These bear very realistic figures that include the Greek gods Dionysus (the Roman Bacchus), Aphrodite (the Roman Venus), and others. One painting in the room is of special interest. It shows what at first glance appear to be two women conversing. Because the artist is long since dead, it is unclear who he meant these figures to be. But one popular theory is that one is the infamous Greek queen of Egypt, Cleopatra, and the other is her Roman lover Marcus Antonius; in this view, when Antonius abandoned Rome for Cleopatra, he left behind his manhood and so is portrayed as a woman. The villa also has several huge paintings showing scenes of temples and other buildings, all done in fine perspective, so that you feel as though you are seeing them through an open window!

Mt. Vesuvius was once covered by dense forests in which the early inhabitants of the region hunted wild boar. Today, however, only a few patches of forest remain. And most of the slopes are covered with vineyards and olive groves. These are among the most lush and prosperous in the known world and are worth seeing. It is also worth trekking to the summit of the mountain, from which the view of the Gulf of Cumae and the surrounding region is breathtaking.

## Herculaneum and Neapolis

From the bottom slopes of Vesuvius, the next stop is the picturesque town of Herculaneum ("City of Hercules"), located on the gulf about ten miles northwest of Pompeii. Like Pompeii, it was long ago inhabited by Oscans, Etruscans, and Samnites before becoming a Roman town. Considerably smaller than Pompeii, Herculaneum has only four or five thousand full-time inhabitants. But it is nonetheless an important Campanian town because well-to-do Romans from across Italy have come to see it as a resort. Not surprisingly, therefore, the town has several large and beautiful townhouses and villas. And for the convenience of the rich, it also has a basilica, a theater, a sports center, a library with an extensive collection of books, and two very nice bathhouses. Unfortunately, the quake of 62 damaged large portions of Herculaneum. Yet rebuilding efforts are ongoing, and one will not be disappointed in spending an afternoon there.

*This is an artist's impression of Herculaneum, the "City of Hercules," which lies about ten miles from Pompeii.*

Only a few miles farther up the coast, one comes to Neapolis, another popular resort town with well-to-do and retired Romans. As Strabo wrote:

Neapolis has springs of hot water and bathing-establishments that are not inferior to those at Baiae [another Campanian town, renowned for its natural springs and baths], although it is far short of Baiae in the number of people. . . . And greater vogue is given to the Greek mode of life at Neapolis by the people who withdraw thither from Rome for the sake of rest—I mean the class who have made their livelihood by training the young, or still others who, because of old age or infirmity, long to live in relaxation; and some of the Romans, too, taking delight in this way of living and observing the great number of men of the same culture as themselves sojourning there, gladly fall in love with the place and make it their permanent abode.[26]

Among the notables who fell in love, as Strabo puts it, with Neapolis, was the great poet Virgil. He studied there under the philosopher Siro and later inherited the older man's local villa, which is now a popular tourist destination. Also, the popular poet Statius was born in Neapolis.

Two other Roman notables who enjoyed Neapolis were none other than the emperors Augustus and Nero. Greek-style athletic games began to be held there in Augustus's honor while he was still living. And Nero made his first stage appearance in the town. Later, after competing in the Olympic Games in Greece (a silly affair in which he lost, but because he was the emperor received the victor's prize anyway), he made a triumphant entry into Neapolis.

## Strabo Describes Neapolis

This tract about the town of Neapolis, from Strabo's *Geography*, emphasizes its athletic games and a tunnel connecting the town to Puteoli.

Very many traces of Greek culture are preserved [in Neapolis]—gymnasia, exercise grounds, and Greek names of things, although the people are Romans. And at the present time a sacred [athletic] contest [initiated in the reign of Augustus] is celebrated among them every four years, in music as well as gymnastics; it lasts for several days, and vies with the most famous of those celebrated in Greece. Here, too, there is a tunnel—the mountain between Dicaearchia [Puteoli] and Neapolis having been tunneled like the one leading to Cumae, and a road having been opened up for a distance of many stadia that is wide enough to allow teams going in opposite directions to pass each other. . . . Furthermore, Neapolis has springs of hot water and bathing-establishments that are not inferior to those at Baiae.

## Puteoli's Port and Clay Deposits

Traveling a few miles farther up the coast from Neapolis, you will reach Puteoli, which many centuries ago went by the name of Dicaearchia. According to Strabo:

In earlier times it was only a port-town of the Cumaeans, situated on the brow of a hill, but at the time of Hannibal's expedition [late third century B.C.] the Romans settled a colony there, and changed its name to Puteoli [meaning "Little Wells"] from the wells there—though some say that it was from the foul smell of the waters, since the whole district, as far as Baiae and Cumae, has a foul smell, because it is full of sulfur and fire and hot waters. And some believe that it is for this reason that the Cumaean country was called "Phle-gra" [after a place in Greece said to be the site of an ancient battle between gods and giants] and that it is the wounds of the fallen giants, inflicted by the thunderbolts [of the god Zeus], that pour forth those streams of fire and water.[27]

By the beginning of the second century B.C., Puteoli had become an important trading center and port, the biggest in Italy in fact. Grain and papyrus from Egypt and foodstuffs and luxury goods from nearly every other region of the Mediterranean sphere flowed into the port. From there, these commodities were carried overland to Rome, Capua, Neapolis, and other cities. In the 40s A.D., of course, the emperor Claudius opened the port of Ostia, farther north and nearer to Rome; and this reduced the importance of Puteoli as a port city. However, Puteoli still imports large quantities of goods used in Campania. The town is also known for its amphitheater, which seats nearly forty thousand people, and fine bathhouse.

Perhaps Puteoli's greatest claims to fame, however, are its rich deposits of volcanic clay, called *pulvis Puteolanus*. These constitute the key ingredient of concrete, the strong and durable substance that has allowed the Romans to become the greatest builders in history. A few centuries ago, some Roman contractors found that adding *pulvis Puteolanus* to lime, in a ratio of two or three to one, along with water, produces a mortar of rocklike hardness.

The mortar is then combined with coarse sand and gravel. Usually, builders lay down a layer of wet mortar, press in a layer of gravel, lay down more mortar, add another level of gravel, and so forth. They keep this up until they have created the desired thickness of concrete.

## Misenum, Cumae, and Capua

Not far beyond Puteoli lies Misenum, a lofty promontory that marks the northernmost edge of the Gulf of Cumae. The area is dominated by three very old volcanic craters, which make it physically

*Two boys carry home an amphora of oil. Many of the goods that arrive on ships at the docks at Puteoli are stored in such containers.*

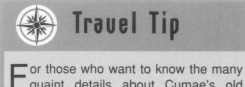

## Travel Tip

For those who want to know the many quaint details about Cumae's old priestesses and their prophecies, local guides can be hired in the town.

imposing and quite a stunning sight, especially at sunrise and sunset. Misenum has two fine harbors that were used for a long time by nearby Cumae when it was a Greek city. Later, in the reign of the first emperor, Augustus, the Roman navy took over these harbors and a port town rapidly grew up near them. (One harbor is now used for naval training exercises, the other mainly for repairs and storage.) The officer presently in charge of the base is the noted scholar and encyclopedist Pliny the Elder, who has a fine villa in the area.

The next place to visit on the coast is Cumae, lying only a few miles north of Misenum and Puteoli. In very early times, Cumae was best known as the site of the cave of the Sibyl, the prophetess said to have guided the hero Aeneas (founder of the Roman race) down into the Underworld. The cave (or at least one purported to be the genuine one) attracts numerous visitors each year. It contains various chambers, galleries, doors, and pools of water, most of these pre-

sumably added long after the original Sibyl departed.

If you have the time, you can make the journey from Cumae to Capua, lying about twenty miles inland. On the Via Campania, the most direct and fastest route, even walking at a leisurely pace one can make it in about five hours. A center for metalworkers and other craftspeople, Capua has

*The cave of the Sibyl, at Cumae, is renowned throughout the Mediterranean world.*

become one of Italy's wealthiest and most prosperous cities. It is also known for its perfumes, made from secret blends of wild roses and olive oil. These are available in the town's many stores, which provide a shopping experience almost as varied as that of Pompeii.

While in town, one can also view the outside of the old gladiator barracks from which the infamous Spartacus launched his rebellion. There is a well-built amphitheater nearby. However, gladiatorial fights are so popular in this region that this arena is always overflowing; and there is constant talk about replacing it with a much bigger one. This is a very expensive proposition, of course, so there is no telling when such a venture will come to pass.[28]

Having seen Capua, the visitor to Campania can either return to Pompeii or head directly home, wherever that might be. Even if one chooses the latter, it is a good bet that he or she will return at a later date. Pompeii and the lovely towns and countryside surrounding it are special places indeed, and those who have had the good fortune to experience them always long to come back.

# Notes

## Introduction: A Note to the Reader

1. Pliny the Younger, *Letters*, published as *The Letters of the Younger Pliny*, trans. Betty Radice. New York: Penguin, 1969, pp. 166–68.
2. Jarrett A. Lobell, "Voices from the Ashes," *Archaeology*, July/August 2003, p. 31.

## Chapter 1: A Brief History of Pompeii

3. Tacitus, *The Annals*, published as *The Annals of Ancient Rome*, trans. Michael Grant. New York: Penguin, 1989, pp. 321–22. Note that Tacitus is not named in the text as the writer in question. This is because he actually wrote this account a few years *after* Pompeii's destruction. The author of this fictional travel guide could not have quoted him, therefore; however, Tacitus's words are included here (and elsewhere in the text) because a real ancient Roman account of the incident adds authenticity and color.
4. Seneca, *Natural Questions*, vol. 2, trans. T.H. Corcoran. Cambridge, MA: Harvard University Press, 1972, pp. 127–29.
5. Seneca, *Natural Questions*, p. 205.

## Chapter 2: Physical Setting and Weather

6. Strabo, *Geography*, vol. 2, trans. H.L. Jones. Cambridge, MA: Harvard University Press, 1969, p. 53.

## Chapter 3: Transportation and Lodging

7. The region encompassing what are now France and Belgium.
8. What is now Turkey.
9. Quoted in Jo-Ann Shelton, ed., *As The Romans Did: A Sourcebook in Roman Social History*. New York: Oxford University Press, 1988, p. 330.
10. Quoted in Lionel Casson, *Travel in the Ancient World*. Baltimore: Johns Hopkins University Press, 1994, p. 204.
11. Quoted in Shelton, *As the Romans Did*, p. 68.

## Chapter 4: Restaurants and Food

12. Quoted in Casson, *Travel*, p. 213.
13. Quoted in Shelton, *As the Romans Did*, p. 329.
14. Quoted in Casson, *Travel*, p. 214.

## Chapter 5: Bathing and Exercise Facilities

15. Modern excavators found the remains of several members of a construction crew that was repairing the bathhouse at the time that Mt. Vesuvius erupted.
16. Due to the eruption and the destruction of the city, the Central Baths never fully opened for business.
17. Oiling and strigiling were then the standard way of cleaning the body.

An early form of soap was already in use in Germany and other Celtic lands but had not yet caught on in a big way with the Greeks and Romans.

## Chapter 6: Exchanging Money and Shopping

18. Quoted in Shelton, *As the Romans Did*, p. 71.
19. Quoted in William S. Davis, ed., *Readings in Ancient History: Illustrative Extracts from the Sources*, vol. 2. Boston: Allyn and Bacon, 1913, p. 265.

## Chapter 7: The Amphitheater and Public Games

20. Livy, *The History of Rome from Its Foundation*, excerpted in *Livy, Vol. 2*, trans. Canon Roberts. New York: E.P. Dutton, 1912, p. 125.
21. Vitruvius, *On Architecture*, vol. 1, trans. Frank Granger. Cambridge, MA: Harvard University Press, 1962, p. 255.

22. Quoted in Shelton, *As the Romans Did*, p. 344.
23. Quoted in Shelton, *As the Romans Did*, p. 344.
24. Quoted in Shelton, *As the Romans Did*, p. 345.

## Chapter 8: Things to See and Do in Pompeii

25. Pompeii's new Temple of Venus never rose any higher than its column bases, as the eruption of A.D. 79 permanently halted construction.

## Chapter 9: Day Trips to Nearby Towns and Sights

26. Strabo, *Geography*, p. 72.
27. Strabo, *Geography*, p. 78.
28. A new and much bigger Capuan amphitheater, second in size only to the Colosseum in Rome, did replace the older one in the second century A.D., about half a century after Pompeii's demise.

# For Further Reading

**Books**

Giovanni Caselli, *In Search of Pompeii: A Buried Roman City*. New York: Peter Bedrick, 1999. One of the better overviews of Pompeii for young people, with numerous color illustrations.

Peter Connolly, *Pompeii*. New York: Oxford University Press, 1994. Perhaps the best presentation of this subject for young people, it features Connolly's excellent text along with his stunning color paintings.

Don Nardo, *Roman Amphitheaters*. New York: Franklin Watts, 2002. Tells about the origins of the stone arenas where gladiators and animal hunters fought and often died, how these structures were built, and the variety of games they showcased.

John Seely and Elizabeth Seely, *Pompeii and Herculaneum*. Chrystal Lake, IL: Heinemann Library, 1999. A very handsomely mounted study of Pompeii and its sister city of Herculaneum, aimed at young and general readers.

Judith Simpson, *Ancient Rome*. New York: Time-Life, 1997. One of the best entries in Time-Life's library of picture books about the ancient world; this one is beautifully illustrated with attractive and appropriate photographs and paintings.

**Web Sites**

**BSR Pompeii Project, British School of Rome** (www.bsr.ac.uk/pompeiiproject.html). Details the ongoing efforts of scholars at the British School to excavate and study a selected city block at Pompeii.

**A Day at the Baths, PBS Secrets of Lost Empires** (www.pbs.org/wgbh/nova/lostempires/roman/day.html). A virtual tour of a large Roman bathhouse, including recent photos of excavated sections of these structures.

**Pompeii Forum Project, University of Virginia** (http://pompeii.virginia.edu). The official Web site of ongoing efforts by a group of scholars to map Pompeii's ancient forum in great detail in order to learn when and how it was built and rebuilt.

# Works Consulted

**Major Works**

M.T. Boatwright et al., *The Shapes of City Life in Rome and Pompeii*. New Rochelle, NY: Melissa Media, 1999. A well-written discussion of ancient Roman life, with a good deal of information about ancient Pompeii.

Annamaria Ciarallo, *The Gardens of Pompeii*. Los Angeles: J. Paul Getty Museum, 2001. A beautifully mounted book with many stunning photos of Pompeian gardens and accompanying text with useful facts about the gardens and houses.

Elaine Fantham et al., *Women in the Classical World*. New York: Oxford University Press, 1994. Contains an entire and very informative chapter on the women of Pompeii.

Michael Grant, *Cities of Vesuvius: Pompeii and Herculaneum*. London: Phoenix, 1971. One of the best general accounts of the two ancient cities, their streets, shops, temples, citizenry, and ultimate destruction.

D.C. Johnston et al., *Pompeii: The Vanished City*. Alexandria, VA: Time-Life, 1992. This short sketch of the relics and life of Pompeii remains one of the best general introductions to the subject.

Willem Jongman, *The Economy and Society of Pompeii*. Amsterdam: Gieben, 1991. A first-rate overview of Pompeian shops, craftspeople, trade, and so forth.

L. Richardson Jr., *Pompeii: An Architectural History*. Baltimore: Johns Hopkins University Press, 1998. Contains a large amount of information about the layout and buildings of Pompeii.

H.H. Tanzer, *The Common People of Pompeii*. Baltimore: Johns Hopkins University Press, 1939. Though older, this remains an enduring and useful study of the people of the city, based on graffiti found in the ruins.

Andrew Wallace-Hadrill, *Houses and Society in Pompeii and Herculaneum*. Princeton, NJ: Princeton University Press, 1994. A scholarly look at the homes and shops of Pompeii and how they were used.

Andrew Wallace-Hadrill et al., *Unpeeling Pompeii: Studies in Region I of Pompeii*. Rome: Edizioni Electa, 1999. Focuses on what has been learned about ancient Pompeii through studies of a single sector of the city.

Paul Zanker, *Pompeii: Public and Private Life*. Cambridge, MA: Harvard University Press, 1998. Provides a useful synopsis of what is presently known about Pompeii and its way of life.

## Other Important Works
### Primary Sources

William S. Davis, ed., *Readings in Ancient History: Illustrative Extracts from the Sources*. Vol. 2. Boston: Allyn and Bacon, 1913.

Mary R. Lefkowitz and Maureen B. Fant, eds., *Women's Life in Greece and Rome: A Source Book in Translation*. Baltimore: Johns Hopkins University Press, 1992.

Naphtali Lewis and Meyer Reinhold, eds., *Roman Civilization*. Vol. 2. *The Empire*. New York: Columbia University Press, 1990.

Livy, *The History of Rome from Its Foundation*. Books 21–30 published as *Livy: The War with Hannibal*. Trans. Aubrey de Sélincourt. New York: Penguin, 1972; also excerpted in Livy, *Livy, Vol. 2*. Trans. Canon Roberts. New York: E.P. Dutton, 1912.

Pliny the Elder, *Natural History*. 10 vols. Trans. H. Rackham. Cambridge, MA: Harvard University Press, 1967; also excerpted in *Pliny the Elder: Natural History: A Selection*. Trans. John H. Healy. New York: Penguin, 1991.

Pliny the Younger, *Letters*, published as *The Letters of the Younger Pliny*. Trans. Betty Radice. New York: Penguin, 1969.

Jo-Ann Shelton, ed., *As the Romans Did: A Sourcebook in Roman Social History*. New York: Oxford University Press, 1988.

Seneca, *Natural Questions*. Vol. 2. Trans. T.H. Corcoran. Cambridge, MA: Harvard University Press, 1972; and assorted works in *Seneca: Dialogues and Letters*. Trans. C.D.N. Costa. New York: Penguin, 1997.

Strabo, *Geography*. Vol. 2. Trans. H.L. Jones. Cambridge, MA: Harvard University Press, 1969.

Tacitus, *The Annals*, published as *The Annals of Ancient Rome*. Trans. Michael Grant. New York: Penguin, 1989.

Vitruvius, *On Architecture*. Vol. 1. Trans. Frank Granger. Cambridge, MA: Harvard University Press, 1962.

**Modern Sources**
**Books**
Jean-Pierre Adam, *Roman Building: Materials and Techniques*. Trans. Anthony Mathews. Bloomington: Indiana University Press, 1994.

Lesley Adkins and Roy A. Adkins, *Handbook to Life in Ancient Rome*. New York: Facts On File, 1994.

Ian Andrews, *Pompeii*. London: Cambridge University Press, 1978.

Paul G. Bahn, ed., *The Cambridge Illustrated History of Archaeology*. New York: Cambridge University Press, 1996.

J.P.V.D. Balsdon, *Life and Leisure in Ancient Rome*. New York: McGraw-Hill, 1969.

Lionel Casson, *Travel in the Ancient World*. Baltimore: Johns Hopkins University Press, 1994.

Joseph J. Deiss, *Herculaneum: Italy's Buried Treasure*. Malibu, CA: J. Paul Getty Museum, 1989.

Ilaria G. Giacosa, *A Taste of Ancient Rome*. Trans. Anna Herklotz. Chicago: University of Chicago Press, 1994. This is the source of the recipe for egg pudding in the sidebar in chapter 4.

Michael Grant, *The Visible Past: Recent Archaeological Discoveries of Greek and Roman History*. New York: Scribner's, 1990.

Harold W. Johnston, *The Private Life of the Romans*. New York: Cooper Square, 1973.

Paul MacKendrick, *The Mute Stones Speak: The Story of Archaeology in Italy*. New York: W.W. Norton, 1960.

Alexander G. McKay, *Houses, Villas, and Palaces in the Roman World*. Baltimore: Johns Hopkins University Press, 1998.

Donald Story and David Brown, eds., *Roman Crafts*. New York: New York University Press, 1976.

Antonio Varone, *Eroticism in Pompeii*. Los Angeles: J. Paul Getty Museum, 2001.

**Periodicals**
Maureen Carroll and David Godden, "The Sanctuary of Apollo at Pompeii," *American Journal of Archaeology*, vol. 104, 2000.

J.R. Clarke, "Landscape Paintings in the Villa of Oplontis," *Journal of Roman Archaeology*, vol. 9, 1996.

Rick Jones, "Pompeii's Block of Time," *Archaeology*, July/August 2003.

Joseph Judge, "A Buried Roman Town Gives Up Its Dead," *National Geographic*, December 1982.

Jarrett A. Lobell, "Voices from the Ashes," *Archaeology*, July/August 2003.

J.E. Parker, "Inns at Pompeii: A Short Survey," *Cromache Pompeiane*, vol. 4, 1978.

D.P.S. Peacock, "The Mills of Pompeii," *Antiquity*, vol. 63, 1989.

Andrew L. Slayman, "The New Pompeii," *Archaeology*, December 1997.

Elizabeth L. Will, "Women in Pompeii," *Archaeology*, vol. 32, 1979.

# Index

# Picture Credits

Cover: The Art Archive/Bibliotheque des Arts Decoratifs Paris/Dagli Orti

© Archive Iconigraphico, S.A./CORBIS, 14, 35, 81

The Art Archive/Bibliotheque des Arts Decoratifs Paris/Dagli Orti, 20, 25, 28, 34, 36, 37, 38, 39, 44, 46, 48, 50, 54, 56, 73, 79, 89, 91

The Art Archive/Dagli Orti, 43, 99, 100

The Art Archive/Musee de Louvre, Paris/Dagli Orti, 94, 97

The Art Archive/Museo della Civita Romana, Rome/Dagli Orti, 57, 83

The Art Archive/Villa of the Mysteries Pompeii / Dagli Orti, 95

© Bettmann/CORBIS, 9, 77, 84

Connolly through akg-images, 13, 41, 47, 61, 65, 68, 88

Werner Forman/Art Resource, NY, 31

© Mimmo Jodice/CORBIS, 33, 36, 40, 42, 45, 76

The Library of Congress, 18

© Lonely Planet, 10, 60, 89

The Museum of Fine Arts, Boston, 71

North Wind Picture Archives, 16, 19, 26, 32, 53, 72

© Vince Streano/CORBIS, 7

Steve Zmina, 23, 29

# About the Author

Classical historian Don Nardo has published many volumes about ancient Roman history and culture, including *The Age of Augustus, Life of a Roman Gladiator, Life of a Roman Slave*, the five-volume *Library of Ancient Rome*, and Greenhaven Press's *Encyclopedia of Greek and Roman Mythology*. Mr. Nardo also writes screenplays and teleplays and composes music. He lives in Massachusetts with his wife, Christine.